PARTICIPATORY AND RESILIENT URBAN GOVERNANCE: THE CASE OF ANKARA CITIZEN COUNCIL

Savaş Zafer ŞAHİN

Introduction and editing by
Feyzan ERKİP

Cover photo © Greater Municipality of Ankara Press Dept.

Cover design by Zeynep Beler

ISBN 9798871138519

Table of Contents

This book is dedicated to all representatives of public institutions, local governments, civil society, professional chambers, universities, and neighborhoods who made sacrifices to make Ankara the center of participatory democracy, sharing, and solidarity culture by rejecting all kinds of marginalization, discrimination, and segregation on the 100th anniversary of the Republic of Turkey and the capital city of Ankara; to all citizens of Ankara who have carried the spirit of Ankara's 13th and 14th century Ahi Republic into the 21st century by taking responsibility and caring about their city as much as themselves; and to all the devotees who have contributed to the existence of citizen councils so far.

Acknowledgements

We are grateful to Aliye Pekin Çelik, Lance Jay Brown and the president Rick Bell who have been very supportive throughout the whole process and all the other members of the Consortium for Sustainable Urbanization who make the publication of this book possible. We would like to express our gratitude to Mr. Mansur Yavaş, Mayor of the Greater Ankara Municipality, for his continuous and sincere support for the Ankara Citizen Council and Mr. Halil İbrahim Yılmaz, President of the Ankara Citizen Council, for his unyielding energy as one of the driving elements behind overcoming obstacles in front of the Citizen Council. We also would like to thank all the people who contributed to this impressive democratic experience by taking part in participatory affairs under official titles or simply as a citizen of Ankara.

Foreword

Rick Bell, FAIA

CSU President

Despite its long history, amazing architecture, and six million people, Ankara is not as well-known as a few other cities in Türkiye, including Istanbul and Izmir. I first traversed the Anatolian plain by train in 1975, thanks to the generosity of a Columbia University Kinne Fellowship. That was the year of New York City's fiscal crisis, when the City was in debt to the tune of $453 million and the famous headline "Ford to City: Drop Dead" appeared in the Daily News. There was a disconnect, to say the least, between national and local politics. Almost as importantly, in 1975 a referendum on the New York City Charter gave land use powers to the local Community Boards that had been created by Robert Wagner and John Lindsay, the better-known predecessors of Mayor Abraham Beame. Beame had won narrow victories in a contentious primary and a four-way mayoral race. With the fiscal crisis spending cutbacks, layoffs occurred throughout the municipal bureaucracy. I saw these up close and personal, having been an intern at the NYC Human Resources Administration (1972-4) and the NYC Department of City Planning (1974-6). Many in Manhattan's Civic Center were fired. Some essential city services and responsibilities devolved to communities throughout the five boroughs. Participatory democracy was characterized as decentralization. What could be done in neighborhoods was debated in the universities, in the halls of power and in the streets.

Savaş Zafer Şahin, author of the book **Participatory and Resilient Urban Governance: The Case of Ankara Citizen Council**, wrote his doctoral thesis on the relationship between urban planning and politics in Ankara and has actively participated in civil society activities and the Chamber of City Planners there. Feyzan Erkip, who wrote an amazing introduction and who edited the book, is best known as a distinguished professor, retired from Bilkent University in Ankara, as well as a correspondent to the Consortium for Sustainable Urbanization since 2017. Her broad-ranging research interests include, among others, urban resilience and governance, participatory planning practices, urban transformations, leisure, consumerism, and environmental psychology. These overlapping strands, from politics to psychology, come together in their book's exemplary history of the Ankara Citizen Council.

As a successful experiment in participatory democracy, the Ankara Citizen Council has eclipsed and inspired similar efforts including those in New York. It is described as "a uniquely Turkish experience" which is "based on the principle of civil society representation" dating back to the Municipal Law No. 5393 enacted in 2004. The number of citizen councils increased significantly in Türkiye after the Local Elections held in 2019. That election changed local politics in Ankara significantly, with the main opposition party, the left-center Republican People's Party (CHP) electing a mayor after five terms of the long-term ruling party, the Justice & Development Party (AKP) of Recep Tayyip Erdoğan. But the book transcends electoral politics to address how thousands of Council participants take direct action, with tacit approval, for everything from resilience planning to disaster relief in Southern Türkiye and from sustainable development to "contributing to common sense in the city." The purpose of the Citizen Council is "to ensure that the relevant duties of the municipality are carried out at the local and participatory level."

But the Ankara Citizen Council does much more, with 23 working groups ranging from public health (especially during the Covid-19 Pandemic) to social innovation, and from urban aesthetics to disaster management, from open green space planning and urban agriculture to neighborhood identity. A list of 110 achievements in an appendix makes the journey to the end of the book a distinct pleasure. I found myself wishing I could simply replace the list's reference to Ankara with an aspiration for the same work happening in New York. Cities learn from each other, and this book serves as a reminder of what we all can do better.

1. Introduction: Inclusive and Resilient Urban Governance

Feyzan Erkip

Resilience: from Theory to Practice

Governments need to be more resourceful and prepared than ever to address the problems in the contemporary city, where the issues are complex and entwined. Global cities became habitats for immigrants from different countries, and their resources were insufficient due to economic and natural crises. Governments must offer versatile public services and be present for all segments of society, particularly for the poor, the minorities, the young, and the elderly. Their perspective of public services influences urban design and planning from neighborhood to regional levels.

Besides, citizenship has evolved into a different meaning; citizens are not solely governed but demand to be considered a part of the governance. They have become more active partners in shaping cities by engaging digital platforms and commenting on provided services. Gradually, along with the Covid-19 Pandemic process, most citizens have become aware that what they do for their benefit will serve the use of the rest of society. Public officials have also understood many ways to facilitate citizen participation. Publicness and the public realm gained importance where local governments must adopt a two-way, mutual relationship to perform better. It needs institutional preparation for utilizing feedback from citizens. Being proactive is the basis for the resilience capacity of institutions.

Presenting perspectives of various global communities, such as the UN-Habitat, the World Bank, and the OECD, concerning urban development would reveal the sustainability concern in their agenda (Serbanica & Constantin, 2023). UN-Habitat (2007) stresses various concerns for an inclusive city, including gender equality and participation by all citizens; Pierre (2019) offers that internationalization can be used for building capacity, which requires multi-level governance in the European Union space. The increasing importance of resilience within their perspective is also visible in most program documents. Similarly, the Rockefeller Foundation's initiative - the 100 Resilient Cities (100RC) - in 2013 impeded the development of such strategies worldwide (Rockefeller Foundation and ARUP, 2015). "After more than six successful years of growing and catalyzing the urban resilience movement, the existing 100 Resilient Cities organization concluded on July 31, 2019". (www.rockefellerfoundation.org). The city resilience index was developed during the project to guide the selected cities (ARUP, 2014). Coppola & Haupt (2020) gave an account of the 100RC initiative and its shortcomings against the diversity of local conditions. They also elaborate on the two new projects based on the 100RC Program - Resilient Cities Catalyst and Resilience Cities Network - as compensation for critiques of the one-size-fits-all approach of the first Program. Fitzgibbons & Mitchell (2019) provided evidence on the biased selection process of 100RC favoring the cities with a more robust resilience-building capacity. Although the Foundation's approach acknowledges the complexity of urban resilience and proposes to work on different aspects, resilience in different urban contexts may have different meanings, where "the relationship between vulnerability and resilience is highly contextual" (Weichselgartner & Kelman, 2014, p.23). Vale (2014) points out the potential difference between 'intended beneficiaries and who benefits' from the results of resilience policies.

Among the cities involved in Rockefeller's initiative, some examples question its transformative capacity and reveal the conditions for transformative urban resilience implementations (for example, see Moloney & Doyon, 2020 for the Melbourne case). One case disassociated itself from the Foundation's approach claiming that it is 'aligned with mainstream approaches to resilience, which are less political, more technocratic and less cognizant of the structural relations that produce the need for resilience' (Roberts et al., 2020, p. 566). Instead, they suggest 'governing resilience from within' by observing specific conditions of a country.

Here, the debate on resilience deserves a brief note. Originating from the ecological sciences, it was first used only in the context of physical structures and disasters. Researchers studying the problems of urban areas eagerly adopted this concept. They started replacing it with sustainability as it seemed to be more promising for complex systems, which are challenging to sustain when facing shocks and threats. Instead, resilience allowed them to discuss the possibilities of continuously recovering and transforming into new forms and structures. Davidson et al. (2019) claim that resilience could be considered 'as a component of sustainability' towards a progressive definition where the complexity of cities necessitates (see also Vale, 2014; Weichselgartner & Kelman, 2014). Rogov & Rosenblat (2018) think that resilience is required to make a city more sustainable, but the reverse is not necessarily true. They (2018, p.6) also claim that 'sustainability sets objectives for a system, while resilience is used to meet those objectives. In other words, 'sustainability prioritizes outcomes, and resilience prioritizes process (but it is not equal to it!) (p.25). Literature on the interlinks and differences between resilience and sustainability extended as broad definitions need to be revised to address urban challenges in practice. Serbanica & Constantin (2023) extensively analyzed resilience and sustainability regarding the geo-location, level of development and type of shocks and stresses using the 100RC database. Fitzgibbons & Mitchell (2019) compared selected cities of the 100RC Program based on their emphasis on social equity and justice. Both pieces of research have invaluable insights into resilience in action.

In this context, resilience became a promising tool for urban governance where flexibility and transformation ease the burden of predicting the change and planning accordingly. However, as Shaw (2012) suggested, the route of facilitating resilience in local government institutions still needs to be clarified. Besides, resilience is a debated concept as transformations favor some actors more than others considering the complexity of contemporary cities and urban governance (Fainstein, 2018; Fitzgerald, 2018). Fitzgibbons & Mitchell (2019) revealed that despite the respect to equity in documents, strategies and actions to identify and improve the conditions of marginalized groups are very few among the selected 100RC. Identifying winners and losers is a serious task that local authorities should undertake. Especially when social aspects are considered, flexible structures which respond to the needs of citizens differently – not equally or on average - are more appropriate for adaptation, transformation and development. The normative aspect of resilience needs to be addressed as a part of the system.

The problem mainly lies in the resilience approaches of urban governments, which need to be more resilient institutions for various reasons. The rigidity of bureaucratic structures in a top-down managerial environment and power concerns make challenging the status quo almost impossible. Thus, adopting the resilience approach is insufficient; the actual task is operationalizing it at the local government level. Marom & Shlomo (2022) point out the need for 'shifting scales and endorsing a diversity of resilience approaches' to respond to specific requirements of different cases. Their approach challenges the top-down central policies and proposes community-based practices and strategies. 'Resilience in action' in that context necessitates better links between multiple sectors and actors and creativity, local knowledge and memory.

After establishing the rationale of the resilient urban systems, we need to elaborate on various forms of resilience in action; understanding the urban systems, analyzing trajectories, rethinking the future and planning for change (Dos Santos & Partidario, 2011). This search for an improved practice necessitates resilient governance in which all stakeholders and actors, local government, NGOs, private businesses and citizens participate within unbiased and just processes. Thus, resilience in practice means operational definitions of strategies, processes and actions, and relevant mechanisms to make applications possible and feasible.

'Operationalizing resilience in practice involves negotiation of the following key framing questions:

- What are the boundaries of the system of interest (which social, cultural, economic, political, or ecological factors are included)? (Resilience of what?)
- Which disturbances should be included in the analysis? (Resilience to what?)
- Which features of the system need to be preserved, which features can change, and what constitutes desirable change (improvement) for whom? (Resilience for whom?)
- What is the time frame for analysis and planning? (Over what time frame)? '(Helfgott, 2018, p. 856)

Considering the main components of urban resilience – among many, robustness, flexibility, abundance, learning from experience, efficiency, diversity, and preparedness may be named – it is challenging to perform all of these in the complexity of urban environments and the dynamic structure of citizens' needs. There is considerable evidence on how rapid technological development and its global impacts influence urban life and citizens' expectations. As Johnson et al. (2018) stated, not only disasters but 'chronic maladaptation of urban areas to global change' influence the well-being of urban citizens negatively. They also noted that the perceived quality of life varies across localities.

Thus, knowing how different communities experience changes and crises is crucial for formulating the problem and its solutions (Fitzgerald, 2018). In this context, the questions asked by Helfgott (2018) reflect the normative character of resilience decisions. Multiple stakeholders with diverse worldviews and interest levels change according to the situation. Making urban resilience comprehensive is not a feasible target due to the continuous transformation of urban environments. Each problem requires a unique solution for localities with different capacities and deficiencies.

The complexity of urban processes requires the more active participation of stakeholders, not only in representing citizens and communities but also in the formulation of the problem and alternative solutions. One such case is Lahti – a small town in Finland with 120,000 inhabitants - city center revealing the process of participation of the whole community in a structured manner (Konsti-Laakso & Rantala, 2018). Shopkeepers, property owners, event organizers, and logistic operators participated with different expectations from urban planning processes. As mentioned by the authors, local communities have valuable insights and 'non-expert knowledge' stemming from their site-specific experiences. City organizations, communities and facilitators worked together toward constructing a collaborative development plan for the city center. This task is not easy, but it is worthwhile if experts leave their presuppositions aside and are open to learning from communities. Being open to change is one condition for sustaining a collaborative process in planning. This approach challenges the diminutive citizen participation with predefined rules and choices. Clarke (2017) points out differences between state-centric and society-centric models that affect local governance, both of which have some advantages in a collaborative decision-making process. The technical aspects of a multi-actor collaboration play an essential role in its success and applicability. In that respect, a group of scholars proposes utilizing operational research (OR) techniques to challenge conservative participation processes. We believe that a radical change in urban governance is imperative for urban resilience, and the only way to make this possible is to establish a resilient local government understanding. Another critical point is that governance is not synonymous with good governance, which requires core institutional values (Hendrik, 2014). This difference also invites a discussion on the organizational characteristics of local governments that are imperative for good governance at a more operational level (Bolton & Leach, 2002).

Midgley et al. (2018) suggest a systematic approach to meaningful community engagement within the operational research discipline. The main reason for their diversion from the broader OR is that definitions of community and participation need to be revisited, where the process and location become defining factors for both. Listening to lay people and learning from the process are critical elements of engagement and community OR. Technical aspects aside, the proposed system serves the emergence of a collective problem and boundary definition through which a legitimate framing and action plan could be developed. Articles published on community OR exemplified this approach with different practices from specific locales (Johnson & Midgley, 2018). It should also be noted that communities have different capacities and constraints, and 'resilience is not a cure-all for communities struggling to come to terms with external shocks' (Platts-Fowler & Robinson, 2016, p. 769).

From our point of view, institutional aspects of resilient urban systems are of utmost importance, as the lack of adequate processes is evident. Many scholars give accounts of specific cases where citizen engagement is at the core of the problem formulation, and investing in social capital and capacity building of communities are the primary concerns. (Weaver et al., 2018; Yearworth & White, 2018; Laouris & Michaelides, 2018; Gomes et al., 2018). In each case, stakeholders – business organizations, NGOs, local communities, and universities - share their values and viewpoints to lead the decision-making process with a collaborative action plan. Despite the differences in local specifics, the process always involves interviews and workshops with all stakeholders, where governance is defined as collaborative action (Pierre, 2019). Social media – i.e., Twitter and Facebook – proved valuable tools for gathering community opinion without potential biases that may occur during face-to-face interactions (Yearworth & White, 2018). The potential of social media is promising for the future of the community especially during crises when resilience is required the most. However, it also endangers the involvement of marginal communities, such as the elderly and lower-income groups, by solely dwelling on the ideas of people with access to technological communication opportunities, such as smartphones, computers, and tablets. The use of social media adds biased information gathering prone to diversions of ideological or political influences. It is known that younger generations can spare more time and are more knowledgeable on social media. They can be influenced more easily by social media leaders that they follow.

Articulating local knowledge in an informal learning environment is imperative, yet quite challenging to realize with a top-down governance mentality (Pierre, 2019). As stated by Herron & Mendiwelso-Benedek (2018), the conditions of informal learning practice depend on the context. A 'transformative space' for active citizenship might be any gathering space where local actors – a community leader may be the catalyst – engage in community matters and decisions. A local space for social gatherings may establish the community identity and engagement in local matters. This space is not necessarily designed for this function; a public library, neighborhood café or park might be a place for community activity and meetings (Platts-Fowler & Robinson, 2016).

The critical point here is the local authorities' perspective of citizen participation. Traditionally, participation is perceived as a component of the democratic decision-making process. However, within a top-down process, government authorities interpret community involvement within their political and moral judgment boundaries. As Fitzgibbons & Mitchell (2019) found out, collaboration means the engagement of stakeholders with representation in the power structure for some city authorities. Underrepresented citizens' voices cannot be heard if their daily life is out of particular concern. Formal community organizations are formed by more active citizens – with opportunities to raise their voices and make demands from local governments. Gomes et al. (2018) state that knowledge-sharing practices may be an additional source of inequality and marginalization if local community members are not evenly represented. Unless a bottom-up perspective is adopted, the resources of local governments are allocated unevenly in favor of organized citizens. A bottom-up approach to governance requires an impartial and informal learning process, including the local authority, researchers and citizens. There are such examples, although limited, of local governments' concern for 'procedural justice' to sustain inclusive actions (Hendriks, 2014).

The technical aspect of knowledge co-production and transformative aspects of collective decision-making is full of obstacles. However, we have potential tools developed by various disciplines, particularly management science and OR (Bammer, 2018). In any case, projects based on case studies are good starting points to assess their applicability. It is understandable that when the crisis is of an environmental or technical nature, it is more feasible to develop quantitative measures for the system's resilience. There are also social issues to be addressed by community engagement to be understood by qualitative approaches. Understanding and defining the problem is the first step to effective collaboration and can generate unique models for participation in collective activities and community resilience (Fineberg, Ghorbani & Herden, 2020).

The lack of resilience within the limits of the existing spatial planning system in Türkiye and the case of Ankara

In Türkiye, various institutions deal with spatial planning, and their roles in the hierarchy make holistic spatial planning almost impossible. Eraydın (2013) points out the weaknesses of mainstreaming planning theory stating that it focuses on procedures rather than substance. This calls for a new planning paradigm and a radical change in planning practices. Yaman-Galantini (2020) documented the planning hierarchy in Türkiye in detail. In addition to national development plans, regional plans, strategic spatial plans, metropolitan land use plans and special purpose plans – i.e., improvement tourism, conservation plans – and complementary plans, and revision plans take place in spatial planning hierarchy. As she revealed, there is no resilience perspective in urban planning except focusing on hazard risks in national plans. Thus, she suggested the addition of urban resilience units at every level of the planning hierarchy.

Nevertheless, the main problem lies in the planning approach and problems in plan application. A recent disaster in Southern Türkiye – a devastating earthquake on February 6 - indicated that problems are far beyond the institutional capacity and control over urban development. As suggested by many researchers, planners and professional NGOs encouraging land speculation in urban areas caused an ambitious urban development and corrupted the overall system. The challenges of the Turkish planning system are the lack of sufficient coordination, poor implementation of plans, and reluctance to integrate scientific knowledge and citizen engagement in the planning decisions, which cause severe consequences (Altay-Kaya, 2019). The recent disaster mentioned above is one extreme example of all these negative aspects.

It is hard to define and attain resilience targets in an environment where institutional culture is built around private interests. In that respect, the 'urban regime' of Türkiye has resemblances with Stone's version as 'only a small selection of societal and political elites -the strongest parties with the most scarce and vital resources - survive the process of regime formation' (cited in Hendriks, 2014, p.558). Developing a culture of civic engagement is required to transform the existing urban planning and development paradigm. The involvement of all stakeholders and citizens should be encouraged in a decentralized planning process.

Turkish citizens are not willing to participate in public matters mainly because governments do not encourage their participation. Participation is usually understood as being part of a previously defined process. As Sorensen & Torfing (2018) propose, 'co-initiation and collaborative innovation' is only possible when local institutions and leaders accept the need for change and are willing to challenge the status quo, which gives them power and control over decisions. The tools developed and experienced by community OR would be helpful and observed with the guidance of an expert outside the municipality. It will take time to establish citizen-oriented governance and particular attention should be devoted to this aspect while governing the city.

The concept of governance gained significance with Habitat II, which took place in Istanbul in 1996. The principles of urban strategic planning were first introduced in the 7th Annual Report, covering the years between 1996 and 2000 (yet to materialize and yield to global neoliberal tendencies). In particular, metropolitan cities started to witness the development of shopping malls, office towers, gated communities and large-scale energy and service infrastructure. The lack of sufficient control over investment decisions caused big capital to select the newly developing, most profitable areas across the city to build shopping malls, office towers and large-scale residential complexes. Planning bodies remained ineffective with the existing limited controlling and managerial tools. This situation caused many problems, including traffic congestion along main transportation corridors and unplanned population increase in certain areas that needed more infrastructure and urban services. Ankara had its share of these developments and became one of the arenas of global investments (Erkip & Ozuduru, 2015; Erkip, 2003; 2010; Ozuduru et al., 2014).

Ankara's primary identity is being the Turkish Republic's capital city, representing the formation of a new regime as a departure from the Ottoman Empire. Despite its long history before 1923 – when this small Anatolian city became the capital of Türkiye – the dominant aspect of its identity has started to be established. However, in the

1980s, the new liberal economic regime gave way to global influences, and Türkiye experienced a significant transformation. 'Although planning prevailed as a legal obligation, partial revision plans and plan modifications have become significant means to get around limitations' (Batuman, 2013, p.588).

After this brief history, it can be claimed that many aspects of the urban identity of Ankara have already been ignored by the local government and contested, undistinguished places have emerged around the city. Especially in the last two decades, the remnants of historical Ankara have been ruined with postmodern absurdities, although the local and central government institutions were aware of the impact. As Batuman (2013, p. 588) stated, 'while all cities were ruled in the same fashion, there were also differences resulting from the historical specificities of individual cities' where Ankara served as a significant source of contestation.

Within these two decades, Ankara became the contested space for the very identity of being the Republican capital. It became a target of pragmatic populism of the ruling party and the mayor of the Greater Municipality of Ankara (GMA)[1], representing the same party. The mayor of GMA

---

[1] In Türkiye, starting with the first law of Metropolitan Municipalities enacted in 1984, metropolitan municipalities are called "greater municipality", which refers to metropolitan municipal jurisdiction area. In this text, the terms metropolitan and greater will be used interchangeably.

had monopolistic power, adhering to the social groups voting for the ruling party. Large-scale urban investments dominated the city's development and growth, and the city has expanded to its fringe, leaving inner-city neighborhoods and the city center distressed. The central government got involved in this construction maze via other residential and commercial spaces (Topal et al., 2019). The most common method for such development was building swiftly, without obtaining the consent of local and central governments but having the support of one public or non-governmental body (a ministry, a lobby or a powerful agency). Most of the city's new large-scale complex development rights and construction permits are given after the structure is built. Since the 1990s, the development plan of Ankara has been subject to many partial changes that have altered the major planning decisions of the city. Many cases were opposed by the Chamber of Architects and the Chamber of City Planners and neglected by local government.

Protecting a city's identity seems vital as transformation is inevitable due to global conditions forcing city governments to be more adaptive and resilient. A continuous effort is required to define the components of urban identity while simultaneously establishing a new identity whenever it provides positive inputs for citizens, the urban environment and space. Urban planning should involve strategies that make adaptation possible when necessary. In this way, a holistic approach to urban planning supports individual cities in developing their routes to positive change. The issue to be discussed is building a new identity without unsupported nostalgia. This is the essence of resilience thinking and the most resisted aspect because it is hard to change the status quo, as mentioned above, for many reasons. This rigidity is the major drawback for Ankara. The main problem lies in the implementation due to the rigid structure hindering necessary operations, inhibiting the municipality's resilience and adaptability.

In addition to the rigidity of the institutional structure of urban governance, the three-layer government – central government, greater and district municipalities – and different political parties ruling different levels make GMA's job harder. Besides, the central government hinders the efforts of GMA either financially or legally. Besides, district municipalities might refuse to cooperate with GMA on some critical issues due to political rivalry and the claim of self-sufficiency. Some local municipalities establish close relations with the central government to attain financial benefits, whereas others generate resources to pursue communal activities during crises. Hence, governance culture does not give way to just stakeholder participation. As Batuman (2013, p. 584) reveals, 'traditionally, the results of local elections had always been consistent with the general elections in Türkiye; hence, the municipalities were controlled by the party ruling the country'. However, local governments are submissive regardless of their political tendencies. Currently, the GMA is governed by the main opposition party, whereas the central government is by the ruling party – because of bureaucratic control mechanisms. The submissive attitude is due to the central government's financial control over municipalities. The ruling party exercises this power frequently, especially after 2019 when the local elections ceased its control over the Greater Municipalities of Istanbul and Ankara.

The institutional capacity of GMA needs to be improved in understanding community needs despite the positive attitude of the current mayor due to the need for more flexibility, continuous interaction, and creativity. Collaboration with stakeholders could be more vital since experience and traditions impose a top-down approach in the decision-making process. The efforts to provide for the needs of citizens have been increasing, but local vulnerabilities and the specific needs of different communities should be addressed. This is mainly because of the lack of dynamism at the institutional level (Yaman-Galantini, 2019).

Excessive capacity and alternative resources help cities during crises when conditions change unexpectedly. Naturally, the resources are limited and cannot be multiplied whenever needed. The point is to prioritize the needs and to be flexible in changing the order when necessary. This is extremely important during crises when some citizens or regions become more vulnerable and need a quick response from local governments. The period of the Covid-19 pandemic provided valuable insights into resilience as a strategy since it reminded the importance of social resilience. GMA allocated its computers to citizens who lack this facility and invested in internet infrastructure in some regions (Kavas-Bilgic, 2021). The global character of the Covid-19 Pandemic and the proper use of communication technologies made it possible to share experiences and problems during the Covid-19 Pandemic. GMA utilized this opportunity by initiating a platform for sharing its experiences with forty-three greater municipalities. This way, capital cities could form a knowledge network that lasts longer. This is crucial for continuous and resilient collaboration among countries and cultures (Kavas-Bilgic, 2021).

Turkish people are traditionally altruistic, especially when their acquaintances are in need. GMA behaved similarly to help needy citizens, where the elderly had a priority. Nevertheless, organizing citizens to help each other became necessary when the municipality's efforts were insufficient. This feature can be better organized and used more systematically. As the donation campaigns of municipalities during the Covid-19 Pandemic were not allowed by the central government due to political concerns, they were obliged to act tactfully and felt restricted in helping communities in need. Their primary concern was not politicizing such acts, so they ran these aids through non-governmental organizations. This is a promising aspect of resilience-oriented strategic planning since it involves social capital and traditions. Learning from experiences and traditions is an asset in coping with unexpected changes. The recent Covid-19 Pandemic nourished this aspect of reflectiveness. Some municipalities have the potential to create reflectiveness with participative and collaborative projects in Ankara.

In the years following the 2019 local elections, a previously established participative mechanism flourished in Ankara in the form of the Citizens' Council of Ankara (Ankara Kent Konseyi-AKK), in which citizens take part in discussing Ankara's problems and GMA's agenda. The documents of the Council reflect its willingness to contribute to a culture of collaboration among all the stakeholders in Ankara (AKK, 2020). This willingness calls for using the tools provided by other disciplines, particularly community-engaged operational research (OR). Changing traditional stakeholder participation requires a novel approach to community engagement. GMA provides educational and cultural services to Ankara citizens in various locales, which could also be used as a 'transformative space' with active citizen participation.

Afterward, a democratic process of urban government was partly restored, and the potential for a 'just governance' emerged. As cited by Platts-Fowler & Robinson (2016, p.768-769), 'Members of resilient communities might 'intentionally' develop personal and collective capacity and engage in a bid to influence change, to sustain and renew community, and develop new trajectories for the future'. AKK provided Ankara citizens with the opportunity to form resilient communities. There is also potential for a more resilient Ankara. Our concern is institutional traditions and limitations regardless of political tendencies, despite the importance of an open mind in planning and governing bodies (George et al., 2018). The attachment to hierarchy and bureaucracy goes far beyond the period mentioned above. This negative attitude was built upon a long tradition of top-down decisions of governing bodies, including GMA, until recently.

The priorities of urban governance should be transparent and participative in that all involved stakeholders, including citizens, NGOs, and experts, take responsibility alongside the local government. AKK provided this opportunity and gathered engaged citizens to work on many aspects of urban issues; now, GMA must act to utilize this enormous potential.

Concluding Remarks

Various levels of urban governments and actors should work in harmony in a collaborative institutional environment. This is one of the most complicated aspects of resilience in traditional planning organizations. Bureaucratic routines supported by the comfort of status quo prevent planners and officials from adopting a new mentality. Turkish local governments need substantial adjustment to resilience thinking through revisions in the governance system. Conceptualizing incompleteness is a novel idea that might be valuable for rigid structures (Durose & Lowndes, 2021). As stated by Shaw (2012, p. 294-295), 'a key feature of a resilient urban authority is to allow space for others to develop their resilience, to harness and direct the ingenuity and commitment of local communities and individuals in responding to economic, social and environmental problems'.

Resilience thinking requires questioning this long-term attitude to policy-making at the local level. More importantly, the cognitive style of planning team members affects commitment, where creating style has a direct positive relation and commitment to strategic planning (George et al., 2018). In other words, being open to change and novelty increases the chance to develop and implement urban strategic planning.

In Türkiye, the three-tier government structure, which restricts the autonomy and subsidiarity of local governments, creates an additional obstacle to integrating urban governance. When the government cannot establish subsidiarity through multi-level governance, its actions become generic, not responding to the real needs of the communities. In this process, underdeveloped regions of a city should be prioritized. Local governments can monitor their territories more effectively than central governments, thus adapting action plans according to their needs. Streets are spatial reflections of communities where social needs can be specified. Community OR would help specify the disadvantaged groups, such as youth and the elderly. In many cases, collaborative action through community engagement increases shared decisions' commitment level and applicability.

The performance outcomes are to be defined and understood as a part of the process, not the final product. This way, the 'resilience of what' and 'for whom' questions can be persistent and make the providing institution resilient against ever-changing circumstances. This approach must be beyond political agenda regardless of the political ideologies of governing bodies, mainly local governments. This is the only local governance route with all the stakeholders representing themselves justly.

Efforts to create a different planning culture with the help of a resilient institution, which offers a new form of governance that enables more flexible, multi-sectoral and multi-actor participation deserve attention. This approach is mostly application and result-oriented and mobilizes people with collective work and action plans. The construction of large-scale projects proceeds swiftly through public-private partnerships, disaster management processes are overseen more effectively, and action plans for particular urban issues, such as the construction of roads and infrastructure, are implemented more efficiently.

Documenting the efforts of AKK to enhance citizen participation would provide insightful clues for the future of resilient cities. Resuming its activities in the last few years is sufficient to reveal AKK's contribution to the involvement of Ankara citizens in the urban agenda (AKK, 2020). It is a valuable experience in building a bottom-up governance structure that needs to be improved in many programs for resilient cities.

References

Altay-Kaya, D. (2019). Integrating the resilience perspective into the Turkish planning system: Issues and challenges, Ozdemir-Sarı, B., Ozdemir, S. and Uzun, N. (Eds.) Urban & regional planning in Türkiye, Springer: Nature Switzerland, 213-233.

Ankara Kent Konseyi (AKK) (2020) 2019-2020 Faaliyet Raporu, https://Ankarakentkonseyi.org.tr/sites/Ankarakentkonseyi.org.tr/files/faaliyet-raporu/faaliyet_raporu.html#p=1 (access date: 18.10.2022).

ARUP (2014) City Resilience Index. ARUP Group Ltd. London, 1-81. https://www.arup.com/perspectives/publications/research/section/city-resilience-index

Bammer, G. (2018). Strengthening community operational research through exchange of tools and strategic alliances, Journal of Operational Research, 268, 1168–1177.

Batuman, B. (2013). City profile: Ankara, Cities, 31, p. 578–590.

Bolton, N & Leach, S. (2002). Strategic planning in local government: A Study of organizational impact and effectiveness, Local Government Studies, 28(4), 1–21.

Clarke, S.E. (2017). Local place-based collaborative governance: Comparing state-centric and society-centric models, Urban Affairs Review, 53(3), 578–602.

Coppola, A. & Haupt, W. (2022). Philanthropic Organizations and the Global Circulation of Urban Resilience Practices – The Case of 100 Resilient Cities. In: The Palgrave Handbook of Global Sustainability. Palgrave

Macmillan, Cham. https://doi.org/10.1007/978-3-030-38948-2_167-1

Davidson, K., Nguyen, T. M. P., Beilin, R. & Briggs, J. (2019). The emerging addition of resilience as a component of sustainability in urban policy, Cities, 92, Pages 1–9.

DosSantos, F. T. & Partidário, M. R. (2011). SPARK: Strategic planning approach for resilience keeping, European Planning Studies, 19(8), 1517-1536.

Durose, C. & Lowndes, V. (2021). Why are Designs for Urban Governance so Often Incomplete? A Conceptual Framework for Explaining and Harnessing Institutional Incompleteness, EPC: Politics and Space, 39(8), 1773-1790.

Eraydın, A. (2013). Resilience thinking for planning, in Eraydın, A and Tasan-Kok (Eds.) resilience thinking in urban planning, Springer: Dordrecht, 17–37.

Erkip, F. (2010). Community and neighborhood relations in Ankara: An urban–suburban contrast, Cities, 27 (2), 96–102.

Erkip, F. & Ozuduru, B. (2015). Retail development in Türkiye: An account after two decades of shopping malls in the urban scene, Progress in Planning, 102, 1-33.

Erkip, F. (2003). The shopping mall as an emergent public space in Türkiye, Environment and Planning A, 35(6), 1073–1093.

Fainstein, S.S. (2018). Resilience and justice: Planning for New York City, Urban Geography, 39(8), p.1268-1275.

Feinberg, A., Ghorbani, A. & Herder, P.M. (2020). Commoning toward urban resilience: The role of trust, social cohesion, and involvement in a simulated urban common setting, Journal of Urban Affairs, DOI: 10.1080/07352166.2020.1851139

Fitzgibbons, J. & Mitchell, C. (2019). Just urban futures? Exploring equity in '100 resilient cities', World Development, pp. 122, 648–659.

Fitzgibbons, J. & Mitchell, C. (2019). Analytical framework and data for evaluating a city resilience strategy's emphasis on social equity and justice, data in brief, World Development, 26, https://doi.org/10.1016/j.dib.2019.104328

Fitzgerald, A. (2018). Querying the resilient local authority: the Question of 'resilience for whom?', Local Government Studies, 44:6, 788–806.

George, B., Desmidt, S., Cools, E. & Prinze, A. (2018). Cognitive Styles, user acceptance and commitment to strategic plans in public organizations: An empirical analysis, Public Management Review, 20(3), 340-359.

Gomes, S. L., Hermans, L. M. & Thissen, W.A.H. (2018). Extending community operational research to address institutional aspects of societal problems: Experiences from peri-urban Bangladesh, European Journal of Operational Research, 268, 904–917.

Helfgott, A. (2018). Operationalizing systemic resilience, European Journal of Operational Research, 268, 852–864.

Hendriks, F. (2014). Understanding good urban governance: Essentials, shifts and values, Urban Affairs Review, 50(4), 553–576.

Johnson, M.P., Midgley, G. & Chichirau, G. (2018). Emerging trends and new frontiers in community operational research, European Journal of Operational Research, 268, 1178-1191.

Johnson, M.P. & Midgley, G. (2018). Community operational research: Innovations, internationalization and agenda-setting applications, European Journal of Operational Research, 268, 761–770.

Konsti-Laakso, S. & Rantala, T. (2018). Managing community engagement: A process model for urban planning, European Journal of Operational Research, 268, 1040-1049.

Laouris, Y. & Michaelides, M. (2018). Structures Democratic Dialogue: An application of a mathematical problem structuring method to facilitate reforms with local authorities in Cyprus, European Journal of Operational Research, 268, 918-931.

Marom, N. & Shlomo, O. (2022). Green, Gray, Glocal: Governing urban resilience in the Tel Aviv Metropolitan Region, Urban Geography, published online November 30, 2022.
https://doi.org/10.1080/02723638.2022.2149946

Midgley, G., Johnson, M. P. & Chichirau, G. (2018). What is community operational research? European Journal of Operational Research, 268, 771-783.

Moloney, S. & Doyon, A. (2021). The resilient Melbourne experiment: Analyzing the conditions for transformative urban resilience implementation, Cities, 110, https://doi.org/10.1016/j.cities.2020.103017

Ozuduru, B.H., Varol, C. & Yalciner-Ercoskun, O. (2014). Do shopping centers abate the resilience of shopping streets? The co-existence of both shopping venues in Ankara, Türkiye, Cities, 36, 145-157.

Pierre, J. (2019). Multi-level governance as a strategy to build capacity in cities: Evidence from Sweden, Journal of Urban Affairs, 41:1, 103–116.

Platts-Fowler, D. & Robinson, D. (2016). Community resilience: a policy tool for local government?, Local Government Studies, 42 (5), 762–784.

Rockefeller Foundation and ARUP (2014) City resilience framework, https://www.rockefellerfoundation.org/wp-content/uploads/100RC-City-Resilience-Framework.pdf

Roberts, D., Douwes, J., Sutherland, C. & Sim, V. (2020). Durban's 100 resilient cities journey: governing resilience from within, Environment and Urbanization, 32(2), 547-568.

Rogov, M. & Rosenblat, C. (2018). Urban resilience discourse analysis: Towards a multi-level approach to cities, sustainability, 10(12), 4431. https://doi.org/10.3390/su10124431

Serbanica, C. & Constantin, D.L. (2023). Misfortunes never come singly. A holistic approach to urban resilience and sustainability challenges, Cities, 134, https://doi.org/10.1016/cities.2022.104177

Shaw, K. (2012). The Rise of the Resilient Local Authority, Local Government Studies, 38(3), 281–300.

Sorensen, E. & Torfing, J. (2018). Co-initiation and Collaborative Innovation in Urban Spaces, Urban Affairs Review, 54(2), 388-418.

Topal, A., Yalman, G.L. & Celik, O. (2019). Changing modalities of urban redevelopment and housing finance in Türkiye: Three mass housing projects in Ankara, Journal of Urban Affairs, 41(5), 630-653.

UN-Habitat (2007) Inclusive and Sustainable Urban Planning: A Guide for Municipalities, v.1. An Introduction to Strategic Urban Planning. https://unhabitat.org/sites/default/files/2014/07/A-guide-for-Municipalities-Inclusive-and-Sustainable-Urban-Development-Planning-Volume-1.pdf (access date: 20.10.2022).

Vale, L. J. (2014). The politics of resilient cities: whose resilience and whose city? Building Research and Information, 42(2), 191–201.

Weichselgartner & Kelman (2014). Challenges and opportunities for building urban resilience. A/Z Journal. 11 (1), 20-35.

Weaver, M. W., Crossan, K., Tan, H. B. & Paxton, S. E. (2018). A systems approach to understanding the perspectives in the changing landscape of responsible business in Scotland, European Journal of Operational Research, 268, 1149–1167.

Yaman-Galantini, Z. D. (2019). Catching on "Urban Resilience" and Examining "Urban Resilience Planning", İdealKent, 10(28), 882-906.

Yaman-Galantini, Z. D. (2020) Kentsel Dayanıklılık Odaklı Planlama Yaklaşımının Türk Kent Planlama Sistemine Uyarlanması, Dirençlilik Dergisi, 347-371.

Yearworth, M. & White, L. (2018). Spontaneous emergence of community OR: Self-initiating, self-organizing problem structuring mediated by social media, European Journal of Operational Research, 268, 809–824.

www.rockefellerfoundation.org

2. The Structure and Working of Citizen Councils in Türkiye

Background

Although they are not called citizen councils, it is known that in the 1970s and 1990s, especially within the tradition of social democratic municipalism, structures similar to citizen councils were tried under the names of "Advisory Board" and "kurultay" in Türkiye. However, the Local Agenda 21 Project, launched in Türkiye in 1997 with the support of the United Nations Development Program, played the most influential role in bringing citizen councils to the national agenda. Within the scope of the Local Agenda 21 Project, Agenda 21 Offices were established in some municipalities and "citizen councils" were established with the initiatives of these offices. For a while, citizen councils existed without any legislative provisions.

It should be recognized that the democratic participatory structures that have been established in Türkiye and are the subject of this paper are a uniquely Turkish experience. Unlike the "citizen assembly" structures that have emerged in recent years, especially in Europe and around the world, which are established for local and national policy-making, the experience in Türkiye is one of long-standing, permanent institutional structures based on the principle of civil society representation. Voluntary citizens can also contribute to these structures. In Turkish, these structures are referred to as "kent konseyi", which can be translated directly into English as "city council". However, for those who are not familiar with the Turkish context, this can be confused with municipal councils. For this reason, this paper will use the English translation "citizen council" for the Turkish-specific experience, the possibility of citizen participation and civil society representation.

In real terms, citizen councils were officially introduced into local government legislation with Article 76 of the Municipal Law No. 5393 enacted in 2004. Subsequently, two separate regulations on the functioning of citizen councils were published in 2006 and 2009. With the 2009 amendment to the regulation, important changes were made in the functioning of citizen councils. With these amendments, the formation, duties, working principles and tasks of the citizen councils were changed. In addition, regulations were made regarding the membership of the citizen council and the citizen council president was added to the organs of the citizen council. In addition, the duties and qualifications of the citizen council organs have been changed. Finally, the general secretariat and secretariat services have been made a part of the citizen councils and a new provision has been stipulated that municipalities may provide in-kind and in-cash aid to citizen councils.

In 2012, with the new metropolitan law, which increased the number of greater municipalities in Türkiye to 30, the municipal boundaries of metropolitan cities were extended to the provincial borders, thus expanding the field of activity of citizen councils. It is estimated that approximately 300 citizen councils have been established since 2006. This number started to increase especially after the Local Elections of March 31, 2019. However, there is no official number announced by the relevant central government institutions. The unstable structure of citizen councils makes it difficult to determine and track their exact number. Since there is a complex relationship between local elections and citizen councils. Sometimes existing citizen councils are interrupted after elections, while other times they continue in a stronger form. With the recent increase in interest in local governments, it can be said that citizen councils have also started to attract attention. There are two unofficial supra-unions, the Union of Citizen councils of Türkiye and the Platform of Citizen councils of Türkiye, established to share experiences of citizen councils on a national scale.

After the March 2019 Local Elections, the demand for Citizen councils has increased, especially with the support of opposition local administrators. Especially in metropolitan cities such as Istanbul, Ankara and Izmir, citizen councils have become more active, which has increased the visibility of citizen councils. Citizen councils are now the subject of both scientific research and the activities of civil society organizations. Citizen councils became able to make their voices heard more in the press and public opinion.

Many problems related to citizen councils have been discussed for many years. The most prominent of these problems can be said to be the pressure of politics on citizen councils, the difficulties of citizen councils to remain impartial and independent, the lack of capacity of citizen council components to adopt a culture of participation, the inadequacies of existing legislation for different scales of citizen councils, the lack of awareness and knowledge of the public about citizen councils, and age, gender and occupational inequalities in participation in citizen councils.

Legal basis

Citizen councils are a form of organization for democratic participation formed around the concepts of sustainable development, citizenship law, urban rights and governance. It is simply a participatory consultative organization consisting of the constituents and stakeholders of a city to manage the city with a common mind. The most important feature of this consultative organization is that, although they are located within the established constitutional order, they have the characteristics of a voluntary network that is not based on institutional, legal and legal conditions. The potential and power of citizen councils in terms of democratic participation is closely related to the characteristics and structure of this network. Taking their legal form from the Turkish law of Municipalities, citizen councils operate in accordance with the provisions of the "Citizen council Regulation", which was previously issued by the Ministry of Interior in 2006, amended in 2009, and is currently carried out by the Ministry of Environment, Urbanization and Climate Change.

Citizen councils are established at the level of local governments as stipulated by law. From this perspective, they can also be called democratic participatory area administrations, as each citizen council carries out participation processes within the local boundaries where local elections are held. In Türkiye, citizen councils can be established at the level of metropolitan, provincial and district municipalities. However, the subordinate-superior relations that are sometimes defined between local governments do not exist between citizen councils and the municipality where they are established, or between citizen councils and other citizen councils, and a horizontal and egalitarian relationship is defined within and between citizen councils. There are two unofficial supra-unions, the Union of Citizen councils of Türkiye and the Citizen council Platform of Türkiye, which aim for continuous communication and information sharing among citizen councils based on equal partnership and solidarity.

By definition and according to the legal framework, citizen councils are not organs, branches or operational units of municipalities. Citizen councils are "consultative and advisory" associations at the level of the municipality where they are established. In terms of the diversity of urban elements they contain, they carry out guiding and remedial work on the services provided by the municipality. As per the legal definition, citizen councils, which are established based on participation and do not have legal personality, are a very different and innovative structure within the constitutional structure and order in Türkiye. For this reason, it is thought that rather than being structures rigidly shaped by legislative regulations, a structure appropriate to the unique nature of that settlement can be formed at each local government level in accordance with the principles set out in the legislation. The thirty years of experience of citizen councils confirms this judgment. Everywhere they have been established, citizen councils have differentiated in accordance with the nature of the localities.

General Structure

The establishment and functioning of citizen councils is carried out in accordance with the "Regulation on Citizen councils" implemented by the Ministry of Environment, Urbanization and Climate Change. The relevant regulation stipulates that citizen councils shall be established within 3 months following local elections in municipalities with a call done by the elected mayor. However, although the establishment of citizen councils is stipulated in the Municipal Law, there is uncertainty about the sanctions for failure to establish them. For this reason, the number of citizen councils in Türkiye, which currently has around 1,400 municipalities, has so far only reached around 300 and mostly in large cities and metropolitan areas. It is also known that the citizen councils that have at least a certain history have serious stability problems.

Citizen councils first convene upon the call of the mayor elected because of local elections. The general assembly of the citizen council convenes upon this call and is composed of the members stipulated by the regulation. A council board consisting of not less than three members is formed from among these members. After the council is formed, the executive board, which is one of the organs of the citizen council, and the president of the citizen council are elected. After the local elections, the citizen councils serve until the next local elections, first for 2 years and then for 3 years. As a result of the new local elections, they are re-established following the provisions stipulated. Citizen councils that have completed the initial establishment process then continue their work by making their calls. As a general principle, it is observed that the functioning of citizen councils is carried out simultaneously with local election processes.

Establishment Objectives of Citizen Councils

The founding objectives of Citizen councils are set out in Article 6 of the Citizen council Regulation[2], which entered into force after being published in the Official Gazette on 08.10.2006. These objectives will be explained below:

Sustainable Development

Defined on March 20, 1987, in the Brundtland Report prepared by the United Nations as "meeting the needs of the present without compromising the needs of future generations", this concept implies that economic development will be sustainable by realizing social and environmental elements together (World Commission on Environment and Development, 1987).

At the United Nations Conference on Sustainable Development held in Rio de Janeiro in June 2012, the goals of sustainable development as it is understood today were

---

[2] **Citizen Council Regulation**, Regulation Date: 08.10.2006, *Official Gazette*, No: 26313.

set[3] and it is now desired to achieve sustainable development in line with these goals. The goals of sustainable development, which are among the objectives of the Citizen councils, are as follows:[4]

1. End Poverty
2. End Hunger
3. Healthy and Quality Life
4. Quality Education
5. Gender Equality
6. Clean Water and Sanitation
7. Accessible and Clean Energy
8. Decent Work and Economic Growth
9. Industry, Innovation and Infrastructure
10. Reducing Inequalities
11. Sustainable Cities and Communities
12. Responsible Production and Consumption
13. Climate Action
14. Life in Water
15. Terrestrial Life
16. Peace, Justice and Strong Institutions
17. Partnerships for Purposes

---

[3]Background of the Goals, UNDP Türkiye, https://www.tr.undp.org/content/turkey/tr/home/sustainable-development-goals/background.html (Date of Access: 13.06.2020).

[4]Sustainable Development Goals, UNDP Türkiye, https://www.tr.undp.org/content/turkey/tr/home/sustainable-development-goals.html (Date of Access: 13.06.2020).

In terms of legislation, citizen councils are related to all these objectives in line with the goal of "sustainable development". However, the relationship of citizen councils with sustainable development goals and sub-headings is not clearly set out in the legislation. This is because there is no "Local Agenda 21" type of instrument established after the 1992 Rio Conference and there is no clarity on sustainable development in the legislation on citizen councils. Nevertheless, various citizen councils in Türkiye are trying to concretize this relationship by conducting studies on the "localization of sustainable development goals". When we look at the sustainable development goals, it can be said that some goals are of interest to citizen councils in terms of participation and all goals are of interest to citizen councils in terms of their mandate. However, the question of which of these goals and what kind of duties fall to citizen councils is an issue that needs to be discussed. It can be said that it is vital to realize a transformation in the organization and functioning of citizen councils in line with these objectives.

The Definition of Citizenship in the Turkish Municipal Law

Article 13 of the Municipality Law[5], which entered into force after being published in the Official Gazette No.

[5] Municipal Law, Law No: 5393, Date of Law: 13.07.2005, *Official Gazette*, No: 25874.

25874 on 03.07.2005, defines the law of fellow citizenship as follows:

"Everyone is a fellow citizen of the municipality where they reside. Citizens have the right to participate in municipal decisions and services, to be informed about municipal activities and to benefit from the assistance of the municipal administration. Assistance must be provided under conditions that do not harm human dignity.

The Municipality shall carry out the necessary work on the development of social and cultural relations among its citizens and the protection of cultural values. Measures shall be taken to ensure the participation of universities, professional organizations with the status of public institutions, trade unions, non-governmental organizations and experts in these studies.

Every person who resides, is located or is related to a municipality is obliged to comply with the decisions, orders and announcements of the municipality based on the laws and to pay municipal taxes, duties, fees, contributions and participation shares."

The purpose of the Citizen council in relation to the law of fellow citizenship is to ensure that the relevant duties of the municipality are carried out at the local and participatory level. In this way, citizens living in the same settlement unit will be able to improve their ties among themselves and contribute to the development of the settlement unit with the awareness of fellow citizenship.

There is a significant difference between the culturally defined concept of fellow citizenship in Türkiye and the legally defined law of fellow citizenship. According to the legal definition, everyone is legally defined as a fellow citizen of the city where they reside, that is, where they live. However, due to migration, citizens may also belong to other cities to which they have migrated. However, citizen councils, while considering such belonging, are based on the concept of fellow citizenship based on urban belonging and feelings of ownership. In other words, there is a relationship in the context of civic life. In Türkiye, while there are also associations of compatriots established based on belonging to the cities where families originate, it should not be forgotten that these associations and other civil society organizations should also be based on solidarity with the city in which they currently live.

Especially in the last decade, as Türkiye has been subjected to waves of international migration, a new dimension has been added to the discussion on the law of fellow citizenship. In addition to refugees or legal asylum seekers, the presence and participation of migrants who do not have these statuses in cities has also become a matter of discussion. In this respect, it is observed that citizen councils are discussing the definition of fellow citizenship in its broadest sense and terms of its humanitarian dimensions at the local level, and some citizen councils have established foreigner and migrant assemblies and working groups. In this respect, it can be said that soon, the objectives of the law of fellow citizenship may be addressed within the framework of an "urban citizenship" concept that also considers the phenomenon of migration.

Good Governance

Governance, as defined in Article 4, paragraph d of the Citizen council Regulation, refers to a multi-actor and social partnership-based management approach based on criteria such as transparency, accountability, participation, work harmony, subsidiarity and efficiency. Good governance means the application of all these principles for the benefit of society without any room for abuse.

Accordingly, the purpose of the Citizen council for ensuring good governance will also be to ensure these principles. The citizen council, which has a wide range of participation at the local level, from the lowest level of district and neighborhood assemblies to the metropolitan municipality level of organization, is of great importance in the realization of the pluralistic nature of good governance and the evaluation of elements such as openness, accountability or transparency in the provision of public services. Here, the citizen council's efforts to ensure citizens' participation in decision-making and budget processes and the monitoring of local governments in this regard are important activities.

In general, it can be said that good governance approaches and cycles have been at least conceptually recognized and followed in practice by the private sector, civil society organizations and public institutions since citizen councils were introduced into the legislation. However, it is observed that there are critical views on good governance in general, which makes it difficult to determine the position of citizen councils. This is because, on the one hand, with the proliferation of grant programs in the field of civil society, good governance has been reduced to a purely mechanistic administrative understanding, and on the other hand, there are sometimes justified criticisms about the loss of the importance of participation among governance mechanisms. In the face of these criticisms, citizen councils, which do not have legal personality, are limited in what they can do in this field. Therefore, the concept of good governance is among the areas that citizen councils are trying to open up for discussion.

Ensuring Effective, Efficient and Fair Use of Resources

Another issue that the citizen council aims to realize is to ensure the effective, efficient and fair use of the city's economic, social and environmental resources. By ensuring the effectiveness, efficiency and fair use of all these resources, the relevant local government will be socially audited. As a result, with the increase in the accountability of the relevant local government, it will be expected that the urban culture of local democracy will develop and participation and transparency will be ensured (Köse and Akyel, 2010).

In addition, the citizen council is established by Article 9 of Law No. 5018 on Public Financial Management and Control[6] "Public administrations prepare strategic plans through participatory methods to establish their mission and vision for the future within the framework of development plans, policies determined by the mayor, programs, relevant legislation and the basic principles they have adopted, to set strategic goals and measurable objectives, to measure their performance in line with predetermined indicators and to monitor and evaluate this process." It contributes to the effective, efficient and fair use of the resources of the relevant municipality as permitted by the provision "The strategic plan is prepared by taking the opinions of universities and professional chambers and relevant non-governmental organizations, if any, and enters into force after it is adopted by the municipal council." in the second paragraph of Article 41 of the Municipal Law No. 5393. Although the participatory processes specified in the aforementioned legislation do not directly refer to the citizen council, it is clear that there is a very close relationship and overlap between the founding purposes and working principles of citizen councils and these regulations. In this sense, it would be a meaningful

---

[6] Public Financial Management and Control Law, Law No: 5018, Date of Law: 24.12.2003, *Official Gazette*, No: 25326.

approach to accept the citizen council as a facilitator in all participatory processes that are valid for the effective and fair use of local governments' resources.

Citizen councils are not an inspection and supervision tool in the conventional administrative sense. The contribution of citizen councils in this sense can be regarded as a combination of the improvement approach called internal audit and the understanding of the public monitoring and evaluating the use of public resources, referred to as public audit. In this sense, citizen councils can develop general principles and policies regarding the spending processes, resource allocation and budgeting approaches of the municipality to which they are affiliated. These policies are closely related to the concept of participatory budgeting all over the world, on the one hand, and innovative approaches to public resources, on the other. As the participation experiences of citizen councils develop, it is seen that innovative models are being developed for the use, production and sharing of public resources with the public.

City Vision

Article 76 of Municipal Law No. 5393, which is the most important legal text on the establishment of citizen councils, defines the citizen council as follows "In urban life, the citizen council tries to realize the principles of development of urban vision and citizenship awareness, protection of the rights and laws of the city, sustainable development, sensitivity to the environment, social aid and solidarity, transparency, accountability, participation and decentralization." "City vision" is one of the keys and first concepts mentioned here. Although there is no explanation elsewhere in the Law as to what a city vision is, the current Citizen council Regulation defines the concept of city vision as "democratic structures and governance mechanisms where central government, local government, professional organizations with the status of public institutions and civil society meet with an understanding of partnership, within the framework of the law of fellow citizenship; where the development priorities, problems and visions of the city are determined, discussed and solutions are developed based on sustainable development principles, and where common sense and consensus are essential" and states that this vision should be addressed concerning the concept of sustainable development.

However, considering that a vision of the future associated with sustainable development can have very different economic, environmental, social and spatial meanings for different nations and cities, it is seen that the activities of citizen councils constitute a very important bundle of possibilities concerning urban vision. Above all, one of the main tasks of citizen councils is to ensure that a city vision that will pave the way for sustainable development is discussed through participatory approaches and to institutionalize a continuous and democratic vision debate. It is very important for the citizen council and democratic participation that urban citizens are motivated to dream for the sustainable future of the city they live in and find such behavior meaningful. Only in this way can the policies necessary to improve the current situation be discussed regarding different future alternatives. What is meant here is a spatial and social vision that goes far beyond the political visions of elected mayors and municipal councils, and that will reinforce and consolidate the relationship of political visions with the city.

Citizen councils are not related to issues such as vision statements, which are often encountered in processes such as strategic planning, but to the "creation of a vision framework". The transformation of the vision statement, which is determined in official documents and institutional processes, into a vision framework by the city's public through participatory processes and tools as part of a continuous dynamic discussion transforms the vision statement into a vision framework, and the citizen council is of great importance here. If vision statements can be transformed into vision frameworks, cities can maintain their dynamism in the face of future changes and reassess their visions in a new and stronger way. The vision framework can turn into a process that will guide the implementation and decision-making processes over time, and the results of the implementations require reconsidering the vision statement and framework. This is why citizen councils should strive to keep the urban vision debate continuous, innovative, vibrant and dynamic in cities. The most basic tool for this is the creation of a public space that considers spatial, administrative and social dynamics and where the urban vision is discussed. Only in this way can a proactive and critical vision discussion be constructed, not a ready-made and imitative one, not a narrow-minded one focused on problem-solving. This public space should be an innovative element that brings together communication channels, institutional capacities, experience sharing and urban public spaces.

Philosophy and Functioning

Have's and Have not's

There is a Culture of Participation, Negotiation, Sharing, Tolerance!

Citizen councils invite every citizen living in that locality to participate in decision-making processes in the city. This participation does not necessarily have to take place within the citizen council. They inform the relevant local governments about the issues agreed upon as a result of citizen participation. Citizen councils, which accept the city and urban values as a common denominator, are the platforms where all views on the city are shared and integrated around the emphasis on urbanity. Since citizen councils are organizations above political parties and ideologies, they are a platform for thinking only in the city, with the city and for the city. For this reason, the culture of togetherness is evaluated on the basis of goodwill between people rather than written rules of law.

The Power Comes from the Influence!

The citizen council derives its strength from the fact that it covers all components of the city. To contribute to a citizen council, it is enough to live in that city or even to care about that city. Citizen councils do not exclude anyone for any reason. The main goal is to ensure that representatives of the central government, local government, professional organizations, political parties, universities and civil society stakeholders participate in the governance of the city. Thus, in councils where pluralism prevails, citizens participate in governance with a sense of urban responsibility to realize the most accurate and inclusive local services with the most stakeholders. The recommendations of citizen councils, which function in a comprehensive, transparent and democratic manner, are very important in setting the agenda of local administrations. In this sense, it can be said that citizen councils have a significant impact on the urban policies of local governments. However, this impact is directly related to issues such as the technical and scientific knowledge that can be brought together in the city, the determination and sustainable follow-up of stakeholders, and the inclusion of solutions appropriate to the specificities of the city.

No Legal Entity!

Citizen councils were established to involve all city components in the management of the city. Participation culture and good governance principles are the main objectives of the council. The citizen council operates voluntarily and in line with established basic principles. For this reason, it does not have legal personality in the legal sense in Türkiye. While such associations may have their legal personality in common law traditions, this has not yet been the case in Türkiye.

No Budget/Resource!

Citizen councils are a platform that adopts local governance as a principle, aims to develop an urban vision and citizenship awareness, and builds consensus around urban belonging. The most important input of this plane is urban values and urban responsibility. Due to the nature of their activities, citizen councils do not have a budget and/or any financial resources. Here, citizen councils can be instrumental in spending public resources within the scope of the support determined by the municipalities for their activities defined in the legislation, but they do not make independent budgeting.

No Office/No Position!

Citizen councils do not prioritize office or position. The priority of the council is always the city and urbanity. For this reason, citizen councils adopt an inter-equal structure, not a hierarchical one. Duties such as chairmanship and executive board membership within the council are only an indication of the desire to take more responsibility for the functioning of democratic participatory processes and mechanisms. In these positions, responsibility is based on the joint fulfillment of requirements such as coordination, cooperation and collaboration. Protocol rules and procedures related to daily functioning, which accompany the concepts of office and position, and the use of discretionary rights based on execution are not included in the functioning of the citizen council. Because institutional relations within the citizen council can only be carried out on the basis of tolerance and trust, not sanctions and instructions.

No Enforcement Authorization!

In Türkiye, the executive power to meet local needs is given to local governments in principle by the Constitution. Citizen councils, on the other hand, are not a unit of the municipality as they are not affiliated to local government institutions and are not part of their organizational chart. The function of the councils is limited to providing advice and offering opinions on the services provided, commonizing local needs and aspirations and setting the agenda within local governments. They do not have executive functions such as direct investment, implementation and realization. However, it discusses general problems related to execution and contributes to the shaping of urban policies as a result of generalized participatory discussions.

What are Citizen Councils?

The experience of citizen councils in Türkiye so far allows for the drawing of behavioral and collective cultural boundaries on many issues. In this sense, definitions of what citizen councils "are not" are also very important:

- The Citizen council is not one of the usual and traditional means of creating a space of power and establishing a hierarchy in civil society.
- The Citizen council is not an extension of daily politics, a place where the classic discourses of polarization and polarization are produced.
- The Citizen council is not an organ, a unit, or an element of the organizational chart of the municipality calling for a general assembly.
- The Citizen council is not an alternative to the municipal council or a space for political debate among council members.
- The Citizen council is not a municipality's public opinion support mechanism, or a tool used by the municipality as a screen against public debate.
- The Citizen council is not a platform to create closed and hidden spaces for spending public resources.

- The Citizen council is not a bureaucratic and frozen organizational structure, but a legal entity that creates unequal processes with rules to be circumvented.
- The Citizen council is not a place where people of questionable legitimacy create positions for themselves without being elected or appointed.
- The Citizen council is not a closed-loop business follow-up area where executive authority is delegated without accountability in the name of participation.
- The Citizen council is not a network where the interests of an individual or a particular group are pursued and protected by exploiting the concept of participation.
- The Citizen council is not a new hierarchy, a new top-down power field, and it does not allow this to be built within itself.
- The Citizen council is not just a club of acquaintances where people who know each other come together, nor is it a waiting room for any political structure.
- The Citizen council is a place where urban problems and urban policies are discussed in a way that permeates the entire city. It is not a place where daily political discourses are reproduced.

- The Citizen council is not a place where discrimination and marginalization are repeated under the name of participation.
- The Citizen council is not a place where non-contentious objection and criticism are used for personal ego and reputation building.
- The Citizen council is not a place where crimes against the city are legitimized.
- The Citizen council is not a place where those who produce value in the city feel uneasy, and hesitant to speak out and express their views.
- The Citizen council is not just a structure that moves from general assembly to general assembly and remains as a signboard 365 days a year except for backstage and list rumors.
- The Citizen council is the place for those who say "I have to express myself and this place is meaningful for me", not for those who say "why am I not here", or "if he is here, I am not here", "what is he doing here".
- The Citizen council is not a place for day-to-day, groping, far-sighted and unscientific approaches.

Basic Components

Today, cities are complex, large and crowded structures that contain many different elements. Urban values are inherently differentiated from rural values and have taken on a new form. In crowded and large urban areas, the division of labor has a complex structure. Citizen councils, on the other hand, act precisely from this reality and despite the many complex structures in the city, they include many stakeholders belonging to different dynamics of all social groups. The stakeholders or components of a city can be handled in many different ways according to different disciplines. However, according to the legislation currently in force, the institutions and organizations that qualify as members of citizen councils are clear. In practice, the representatives of these institutions and organizations have the right to participate in the general assemblies of citizen councils, and citizens, along with other institutions and organizations, can participate in all other activities of citizen councils. The difference between "component" and "institutional member" emerges here. All individuals, institutions and organizations that participate and contribute to the work of the Citizen council without any legislative obstacles can be called constituents, and the institutional structures specified in the legislation and entitled to be members can be called stakeholders. Although a complete and detailed ranking of these stakeholders is undoubtedly difficult, the following classification can be taken as a basis:

Central Administration Representatives

According to the Constitution, Türkiye is a unitary state. Therefore, public services for citizens are provided by the central government and decentralized governments. The central government carries out nationwide public services through its provincial and district-level provincial organizations. For this reason, the service area of the central government is also significant in urban areas. For this reason, citizen councils include the highest local administrative authority, or its representative (governor in provinces and district governor in districts) and representatives of public institutions and organizations designated by the representatives of the local administrative authority. According to the Regulation on Citizen councils, the maximum number of representatives of public institutions and organizations can be ten.

Municipality Representatives

Article 127 of the Constitution stipulates that, in addition to the central government, local governments elected by the electorate shall be established to meet local needs. Provided that they comply with certain limits, local governments apply the principle of subsidiarity in service. In this respect, local governments are the closest administrative unit intertwined with the daily lives of citizens. For this reason, local governments constitute an important focus in determining urban problems and agendas. As stipulated in the Citizen council Regulation, citizen councils convene upon the call of mayors following local elections. The Regulation also stipulates that the mayor or his/her representative shall be a member of the citizen council. However, the membership of the mayor does not differ from other memberships except for his/her will to call for the establishment of the citizen council.

Mukhtars

Mukhtars are the heads of village or neighborhood-level administrations. Being the head of a village and neighborhood administration is different. While the village is a constitutional unit of local government, neighborhoods are usually considered together with the municipal administration as a representative of the state at the neighborhood level. However, in all circumstances, mukhtars are the closest authority to citizens. Especially for metropolitan municipalities, the importance of mukhtars in identifying the smallest problems and bringing them to the agenda is clear. The Citizen council Regulation stipulates that in municipalities with up to 20 neighborhoods, all neighborhood mukhtars, and in other municipalities, representatives to be elected from among themselves, not exceeding 30 percent of the total number of mukhtars and not less than 20, shall be members of the citizen council. Following the current metropolitan law, all mukhtars in metropolitan cities, regardless of their rural character, can be members of the citizen council, whereas in non-metropolitan cities, only mukhtars within municipal boundaries can be members of the citizen council.

Universities

Universities are institutions that provide education/training at higher education levels and carry out scientific activities. The value added by universities to cities is multidimensional. Universities change the face of cities with their student potential, contribute to the urban economy with their research and development activities, and provide a cultural change in cities. For this reason, universities become an important symbol for cities. The Citizen council Regulation states that there shall be at least one representative from universities, but not more than two. However, if there is more than one university in the city, one representative from each university becomes a member of the citizen council. Considering that universities include many academics and students as well as faculties, research centers, etc., it is very important for university members to contribute to the activities of the citizen council without institutional representation. Such participation should be supported and encouraged to ensure the contribution of scientific knowledge, especially in the activities of working groups and assemblies.

Associations

Associations are legal entities that operate as a community of people for specific purposes without the aim of making a profit. Associations have an important social quality in terms of the will of citizens gathered for different purposes in the urban area. As such, associations formed with very different subjects, aims and objectives affect urban life. For this reason, the Citizen council Regulation stipulates that representatives of the associations in that urban area can be members of the citizen council without any limit on the number of members. Considering the sociological structure of Türkiye, it is very important to ensure a balance of rights-based and expertise-based associations in citizen councils in the face of the dominance of kinship (hemşehri)[7] associations formed by people who migrated to the city from rural areas. Although there is no complete clarity in the legislation on this issue, many citizen councils try to elaborate on this issue while preparing their directives.

Foundations

Foundations are legal entities that encompass the allocation of certain property and rights to specific and permanent purposes. Foundations represent a centuries-old tradition in Türkiye. Throughout history, foundations have been

---

[7] The term "hemşehri" is a well-known Cultural and social phenomenon in Turkish Cities. As a result of approx. 50 years of migration from rural areas to large metropolitan areas, migrants formed associations to bring together people from the same province, district or even village to form a solidarity and sometimes nepotism network to fight against disadvantageous situations in city life. Yet, these associations, though very influential, are seen as disruptive forces on the way to establish a common city culture and identity in metropolitan areas.

organizations that have observed social balance, especially in areas where the state cannot reach geographically and economically. Therefore, they are important organizations for urban life. The Citizen council Regulation stipulates that representatives of foundations can be members of the citizen council in the same way as associations, with no limit on the number of members.

Trade Unions

Trade unions are independent organizations with both a social and economic dimension, established to protect the social and economic interests of people working in urban areas. Within the urban economy, trade unions are vital for clarifying and reconciling relations between workers and employers. At the same time, since cities have a complex division of labor and a highly specialized working life, trade unions are important spokespersons in this field. Given the massive size of the working population in the urban economy, trade unions are involved in many social issues. The Citizen council Regulation also stipulates that trade unions can be members of the citizen council with no limit on the number of members. Furthermore, trade unions can be members of the citizen council without any distinction between civil servants, employees and employers' unions. However, the fact that there is no distinction between branches, branches, federations and confederations of trade unions in terms of membership to citizen councils complicates the representation of trade unions in citizen councils.

Professional Organizations

Professional chambers are structures established to facilitate the work done by certain professional groups, to ensure solidarity, to advocate for professional interests and to prevent unfair competition within the profession. According to Article 135 of the Constitution of the Republic of Türkiye, professional organizations in the nature of public institutions are established by law and their organs are determined by their members by secret ballot under judicial supervision. Chambers have a great impact on different business and professional groups in urban areas. The Union of Chambers and Commodity Exchanges of Türkiye, Turkish Medical Association, Turkish Dental Association, Turkish Bar Association, and Union of Chambers of Turkish Engineers and Architects are among these professional organizations. For this reason, the function of chambers and unions in setting the urban agenda and their reactions to urban practices are important. The Citizen council Regulation also stipulates that professional chambers can be members of the citizen council without any limit in number.

Tradesmen Organizations

In addition to professional chambers, the origins of tradesmen's organizations can be traced back first to the

Ahilik Organization and then to the guild organizations that began to be institutionalized in the Ottoman Empire in the 15th century. Both types of organizations in the Ottoman Empire carried out activities for the tradesmen in the city to continue their business life with a culture of morality and solidarity. Guilds had an important place in urban economic relations by maintaining their activities in the places where tradesmen doing the same business were located. Likewise, today, tradesmen organizations, particularly the Federation of Turkish Tradesmen and Craftsmen and affiliated federations, work on the same logic and function as the voice of tradesmen, who are important actors of the urban economy, even though the urban scale has grown. The Citizen council Regulation stipulates that tradesmen's organizations can also be members of the citizen council without any limit on the number of members.

Political Parties

Political parties are organizations formed by people with close political views who claim to govern the country. For a democratic way of life, political parties are the most important political tool for people to realize their principles and goals. For this reason, political parties also carry out activities in citizen councils in order to highlight different social views and opinions in urban politics. However, although political parties are invited to the general assembly of the citizen council, they cannot be present as party representatives in the decision, management and working bodies of the citizen council.

Internal Organization

The Citizen council Regulation stipulates that citizen councils may establish assemblies and working groups on issues within their mandate. These assemblies and working groups are determined in line with the needs and demands of the cities. Each representative of the assemblies and working groups formed under the roof of the citizen council on issues and groups related to the city is also a member of the citizen council. Assemblies operate on a wide range of issues related to urban public life, elect their own chairpersons and executive boards, and form their working groups if necessary. Working groups under the citizen council, on the other hand, are narrower groups established for thematic consensus on time-, place- and event-specific issues related to the city. Assemblies and working groups are the main spheres of production and interaction in the citizen council.

The organs of the Citizen council are set out in Article 9 of the Citizen council Regulation. These organs consist of the General Assembly, Executive Board, Assemblies and Working Groups and the President of the Citizen council.

General Assembly

The provisions regarding the General Assembly of the Citizen council are set out in Article 10 of the Citizen council Regulation. This regulation is enacted in line with the Turkish Municipal Law No. 5393. Accordingly, the General Assembly of the Citizen council has the following characteristics:

1. It is the authorized decision body of the Citizen council.
2. Its members are:

- The highest local administrative authority or its representative, the mayor or its representative,
- Representatives of public institutions and organizations to be determined by governors in provinces and district governors in districts, not exceeding 10 in number,
- In municipalities with up to twenty neighborhoods, all neighborhood mukhtars; in other municipalities, representatives to be elected from among themselves by the neighborhood mukhtars convened upon the call of the mayor, not exceeding 30 percent of the total number of mukhtars and not less than 20,
- Representatives of political parties that have established their organizations in the town,
- At least one representative from each university, but not more than two, or one representative from each

university if the number of universities is more than one,

- Representatives of professional organizations with the status of public institutions, trade unions, notaries, bar associations and relevant associations and foundations,
- One representative of each of the councils and working groups established by the citizen council.

3. It convenes with the absolute majority of its members, but not less than two meetings in January and September each year.
4. The General Assembly shall be chaired by the President of the Citizen council. In the absence of the President of the Citizen council, the oldest member of the Executive Committee shall chair the General Assembly.
5. It determines the election and working principles of the Executive Board, assemblies and working groups with a working directive that does not contradict the Citizen council Regulation.

Executive Committee

Provisions regarding the Executive Board of the Citizen council are included in Article 11 of the Citizen council Regulation. These provisions include the following:

1. Elected by the General Assembly.
2. They are elected for two years for the first term and three years for the second term.

3. It consists of at least seven people.
4. It should also include the Presidents of the Women's and Youth Assemblies.
5. The Executive Committee shall be chaired by the President of the Citizen council, and in the absence of the President, by the oldest member of the Executive Committee.
6. It determines the agenda of the General Assembly.
7. It submits the opinions formulated by the General Assembly to the relevant municipality and monitors their implementation.

Assemblies and Working Groups

Provisions on Assemblies and Working Groups in the Citizen council are included in Article 12 of the Citizen council Regulation. Information on these provisions can be given as follows:

1. They can be formed on issues that fall within the mandate of the Citizen council.
2. Working procedures and principles shall be determined by the General Assembly.
3. After the opinions formed in the Assemblies and Working Groups are discussed and accepted by the General Assembly of the Citizen council, they are submitted to the relevant Municipal Assembly for consideration.

President

Provisions regarding the duties, powers and responsibilities of the Citizen council President are stipulated in Article 11/ A of the Citizen council Regulation:

1. Elected by the General Assembly.
2. The term of office shall be two years for the first term and three years for the second term, in parallel with the term of office of the Executive Board.
3. For the election of the President of the Citizen council, two-thirds of the total number of members of the General Assembly shall be sought in the first ballot; in the second ballot to be held in case this majority is not found, the absolute majority of the total number of members shall be sought. If the absolute majority is not achieved in the second ballot, a third ballot shall be held between the two candidates who receive the highest number of votes in this ballot. The candidate who receives the highest number of votes in the third vote shall be elected as the President of the Citizen council.
4. The election of the President of the citizen council shall be completed in the first meeting of the first meeting of citizen council.
5. In cases where the President of the Citizen council is absent from his/her duty due to leave, illness or any other reason, the oldest member of the

Executive Board shall act as his/her deputy for this period.

Working Principles

The working principles of the Citizen council bodies are stipulated in Article 7 of the Citizen council Regulation. However, there are also various principles stemming from the structure and raison d'être of the Citizen councils, discussions on citizen councils and research on good practices. These can be explained as follows.

Horizontal Organization

By adopting a horizontal organization model, the Citizen council activates the principles of solidarity and joint work as a way of working. In this direction, unlike the rigid and centralized hierarchical order, everyone participating in the Citizen council is in a structure that includes the sharing of roles in the work and solving the problem together, not within the framework of subordinate-superior relations. Participants in the Citizen council do not carry out their work for the sake of competition or to gain prestige. On the contrary, the participants, who act with the awareness of producing for the city and assuming responsibility for the city, work in coordination and cooperation. In case individual and community, conflicting interests with the benefits to be created for the city through the citizen council, it is essential to prioritize the integrative structure of the citizen council. Otherwise, the culture of cooperation within the citizen council will be damaged. It is also important that the horizontal organization is based on an understanding that covers different local scales within the framework of the principle of "top-down coordination, bottom-up production, and decision-making in all directions that support production".

Participation starts at the neighborhood and district level

Participation in the Citizen council starts with neighborhood and district assemblies. Neighborhood mukhtars and neighborhood and neighborhood assemblies contribute fully to the council, where participation is essential, and are of great importance in the realization of the desired principle of subsidiarity. Under the leadership of the smallest settlement unit, neighborhoods and districts, active citizen participation in governance is increased and an egalitarian structure is developed. Citizen councils at the metropolitan and district levels cooperate in building this kind of participation. For this reason, a participatory process starting from the neighborhood and district level must be discussed within each citizen council. The grading, form, organization and development of this participatory process in each city may differ according to the characteristics of that city.

Facilitating function of the chair and steering committee

To realize the horizontal organization model and active citizen participation, the Chairperson and the Executive Board fulfill functional duties on behalf of the Citizen council. In this context, the President and the Executive Board, elected to represent the Citizen council, where many different social segments come together, carry out their work to realize the demands and ideas coming from the General Assembly, Working Groups and Assemblies. They do not gain any financial gain while doing so. The Citizen council, which was established under the leadership of citizens working on behalf of the city, is represented by citizens who are active and working for the city by democratic elections. However, when necessary, the chairperson and executive boards can take the initiative to strengthen this facilitative and pioneering function.

Making working groups and assemblies the main production center

One of the most important features of the Citizen council is that the actual production for the city takes place within the working groups and assemblies established within it. In the working groups and assemblies that want to produce for the city and are differentiated according to their subjects and areas of expertise; there is the opportunity to produce for all works that are considered to be beneficial for the city. It should be noted that the source of legitimacy for the content and information produced is not only knowledge and expertise but also a sense of interest and ownership in the problems of the city. However, this principle should not be interpreted as meaning that working groups and assemblies are closed structures, and it should be recognized that the basic principles of the citizen council apply to them as well.

Owning your city

The Citizen council carries out activities to protect and develop the values of the city, which are the common heritage of humanity. In this context, the Citizen council, which protects the historical and cultural heritage of the city, aims to develop the city spiritually and materially. The Citizen council, which carries out all these activities in close contact with the society and conveys the demands of the society to the local government bodies, creates public opinion in order to solve the problems of the city and creates a basis for policy determination.

Partnership in solution

The Citizen council aims to cooperate with public institutions and organizations, non-governmental organizations, associations, unions, trade unions, foundations, professional organizations with public institutional status and the society itself in solving all problems related to the city and to solve problems through these partnerships. In this respect, the Citizen council, which consists of components that not only benefit from the solution of the problem but also contribute to the solution of the problem, provides the appropriate environment for all segments of society to contribute to the problem to be solved.

Neutrality

The Citizen council does not discriminate either politically or socially in its functions. Citizens from all segments of society to the extent that they wish to participate, have a say in decisions and activities for the benefit of the city as part of this structure. In the Citizen council, where working groups and assemblies are also organized based on impartiality, only positive discrimination is applied to women, children, youth and disabled people by Article 10 of the Constitution of the Republic of Türkiye and Article 6, paragraph (ğ) of the citizen council Regulation.

Innovation

The Citizen council strives to realize all kinds of innovations that can be implemented for the benefit of the city. In this context, the Citizen council supports innovations that will contribute to the development of the city and children and young entrepreneurs who can realize these innovations. Since citizen council activities also have the potential to generate many externalities such as employment, solution of social problems, and economic and spatial development in the city, innovative activities and ideas in this sense contribute to the whole city.

Result-oriented working

The Citizen council works to achieve results that will benefit the city, not for the sake of procrastination or lack of solutions. Moreover, due to its cooperation with all segments of society, it accelerates the decisions that can be taken on behalf of the city and supports practices that benefit citizens. However, result-orientedness should not be interpreted as "the necessity of reaching a result" and the responsibility of the citizen council, which should not be the responsibility of the citizen council but of the institutions with authority, should be well defined.

Activities of Citizen Councils

In line with the broad definition in the legislation, citizen councils can carry out activities in many areas. The source of these activities is the citizens who carry out activities in the citizen council voluntarily. In this sense, citizens can carry out technical, cultural, social, artistic and many other types of activities through citizen councils:

- Discussing urban problems
- Conducting studies on urban policies
- Contributing to common sense in the city
- Contributing to the participatory and accountable functioning of local government

- Making studies on urban culture, belonging and urban identity
- Contributing to the self-expression of interest groups in the city
- To protect the natural and cultural environment of the city
- Conducting studies on urban rights
- Contributing to sustainable development in the city
- Addressing problems in urban transportation
- To ensure the coordination of participation of institutions and organizations in the city
- Supporting city-specific artistic activities
- Promoting and protecting the city's geographically marked products
- Making the voices of innovative ideas in the city heard
- Conducting awareness studies on urban public spaces
- To strive for the development of the capacity and quality of participation in the city
- To cooperate with other Citizen councils
- Organizing solidarity in the city in disasters and other situations

References

Köse, H. Ö. and Akyel, R. "The Search for Efficiency in Public Administration: The Necessity of Effective Audit for Effective Public Administration", *Turkish Administrative Journal*, Year: 82, Issue: 466, 2010, p. 34.

World Commission on Environment and Development, **Our Common Future**, Turkish Environmental Problems Foundation Publications, 1987, Ankara, pp. 23-31.

3. The Experience of Ankara Citizen Council

Pre-2019 Experience

Ankara constitutes an interesting example in terms of participation in urban governance and citizen councils. In the 1970s and 1990s, there were some attempts at participation carried out by social democratic municipal administrations. However, despite being the capital of the National Assembly where Local Agenda 21 and similar frameworks were adopted, the existence of various civil society organizations that have worked on these principles in depth, the high level of education and many other factors, participatory practices have not developed significantly in Ankara, especially in the last two decades. Participatory mechanisms have not emerged to overcome the deficiencies of local representation channels, which have been insufficient in the face of the escalation of socio-economic segregation and polarization in the city in recent years. A significant representation-participation vacuum continues to exist in the city of Ankara (see also Şahin, 2011). Although one might think that citizen councils would constitute an important channel of participation in the face of this situation, this has not been the case. Before 2006, when the Regulation on Citizen councils was first enacted, there were a few weak Local Agenda 21 attempts and Local Agenda 21 Representative Offices were opened. Although civil society organizations in the city have been active in establishing two informal "citizen councils" indirectly related to Local Agenda 21, these activities have not been institutionalized. Platform-type civil society formations, which oppose various practices of city administrations and are mostly led by professional chambers affiliated to the Turkish Association of Chambers of Architects and Engineers (TMMOB) and trade unions, have also not been institutionalized in this sense.

The first citizen councils in Ankara were established after the Regulation on Citizen councils came into force. However, it is observed that these citizen councils did not have serious effectiveness and weight. In 2009, after the amendment of the Regulation on Citizen councils, citizen councils became a part of candidates' programs during local elections. The number of citizen councils has increased. In 2010, 19 out of 46 municipalities in Ankara Province had citizen councils. Ten years later, with the Metropolitan Municipality Law No. 6360, the number of municipalities in Ankara decreased to 25, and the number of municipalities with active citizen councils was limited to 8. This shows that there has been no significant improvement in the status of citizen councils in Ankara over the past decade. It is observed that most of the citizen councils are established by district municipalities within the borders of greater municipalities. Some district municipalities outside the greater municipality boundaries have also established citizen councils. Most of these citizen councils were established in accordance with the Regulation on Citizen councils of 2009. Even if some of them are associated with Local Agenda 21, this relationship is very weak.

From past to present, most of the citizen councils in Ankara have been chaired by mayors, deputy mayors, vice mayors and citizen council members. This situation, which raises serious questions about the autonomy of citizen councils, has been presented in public statements as cooperation between the municipality and the citizen council, and in many statements, the citizen council has been introduced as a tool for municipalities to find "new ideas" and "innovations". This approach, in which citizen councils are presented as instruments of municipalities, is incompatible with the purpose of the establishment of citizen councils. A similar situation is observed in the executive boards, women and youth assemblies and working groups of citizen councils. In the majority of citizen councils, it is observed that the majority of the management of these bodies is composed of the municipality's administration, or of the proxy civil society organizations set up by people close to the municipality's administration. The narrowness of participation in citizen council activities is effective in this sense. In many citizen councils, working groups remain on paper and do not work.

Again, it is observed that almost all citizen councils do not make any effort to form an organization at the district or neighborhood level. Similarly, it is observed that the citizen councils have very low levels of implementation of participatory methods in their internal practices and activities and that their capacity for participation is low. As can be seen, the level of effectiveness of the citizen councils in Ankara has been limited due to their political positioning, and the contribution of the citizen council experience to participatory urban governance at the local level has been realized at a low level. The primary reason for this is that citizen councils in Ankara are perceived and structured as natural extensions of municipalities[8].

---

[8] In this sense, Ankara Citizen council, established by the Greater Municipality of Ankara in 2014, is a striking example. The majority of its executive board members are Municipality bureaucrats and council members, and some of them are representatives of seriously controversial civil society organizations. For instance, the head of the citizen council, was a member of the Municipal Assembly for twenty-four years, during most of which time he was the chairman of the Zoning, Public Works and Naming Commission and deputy mayor. He has frequently come to the fore in Ankara, especially with his efforts to name the street he lives on after himself. As a result of these efforts, he was the subject of judicial processes with the citizens in his neighborhood. Apart from this, the same person was criticized for his secret relations and corruption practices especially in urban planning processes and identified with anti-participatory municipal administration. It is striking that such a person is became the head of the citizen council.

Experience after the 2019 Local Elections

There have been previous attempts to establish metropolitan-scale citizen councils in the capital Ankara. In 2009 and 2014, after the local elections, citizen councils were established with the influence of people who had previously or currently served in the municipality. However, these citizen councils have not achieved sufficient recognition and widespread influence. However, the 2019 local elections in Türkiye have created new hope for citizen councils in Ankara in two ways. First, political parties, without exception, devoted significant space to participation and citizen councils in their election manifestos. Secondly, 11 of the 30 metropolitan municipalities, including Ankara and Istanbul, were won by the opposition, creating a new and competitive environment for gaining legitimacy at the local government level.

After the 2019 local elections, the Greater Ankara Municipality brought participation, transparency and common sense to the agenda, and considering the key role of the citizen council in achieving these goals, it has come to the agenda to revitalize Ankara Citizen Council with an understanding in line with new and contemporary approaches. In this context, Ankara Citizen council held its first general assembly on June 29, 2019, and started its activities. An open call was made for the general assembly and universities, governorship, mukhtars, political parties, associations and foundations, trade unions, professional chambers and tradesmen's chambers, which have the right to participate in the general assembly of the citizen council in accordance with the legislation, were invited. 270 institutions and organizations participated in the general assembly, which elected the president of the citizen council and a 21-member executive board. Ankara Citizen Council, which has largely completed its establishment and institutionalization phase in the past four years, has opened its doors to all citizens and stakeholders of the city according to the inclusive governance approach, and as a result, it has made significant progress in the name of participatory democracy and urban diplomacy in the capital Ankara with nearly 1700 members, more than 5000 volunteers, nearly 30 working groups and 5 councils. Ankara Citizen council has today become the most widely participatory citizen council in Türkiye, with all kinds of participants coming together in participatory activities being called "constituents"[9] . In the case of the capital Ankara, there has never been a citizen council of this scale before. Although the establishment process was not smooth, with this experience, Ankara has begun to have a

---

[9] In physics and chemistry, each of the forces or substances of different directions and intensities that make up a force or compound is called a "component". In social sciences, every element that contributes to a common public framework is called a "component". All stakeholders of the city council can be called a component by creating and contributing to the institutional framework of the city council while maintaining their own activities and uniqueness.

significant awareness of citizen councils on a capital city scale.

Citizen councils have three main tasks. These can be summarized as creating a common mind with a participatory approach in the sustainable development process of the city and matters concerning the law of citizenship, contributing to the realization of a participatory, transparent and accountable local governance process, and establishing the infrastructure of participation and negotiation processes to protect the public quality of the city. In Ankara Citizen Council, the main duties of the chairperson and the executive board of the citizen council are to act as secretariat and facilitator for all institutions and organizations participating in the work of the citizen council, to facilitate the establishment of relations with local governments regarding the priorities of the citizen council components and to support institutional collaborations. For this reason, it is constantly emphasized that the citizen council is a new-generation organization that has no budget, legal personality, office or position, which carries out its activities entirely on a voluntary basis, and that derives its power from its influence based on participation. This kind of organization has the potential to be a source of hope that strives together with the citizens to create a livable and sustainable urban life for all.

Within the citizen council, the work that will create the common mind of the city and raise public awareness of the priorities of the city is mainly carried out by structures called working groups and assemblies. Through the work of these structures with specialized knowledge and technical know-how, advisory decisions can be created and forwarded to the municipal council. It is a legal obligation for these recommendations to be included on the agenda of the first council meeting. After its establishment, Ankara Citizen Council submitted recommendations to the Greater Ankara Municipality Assembly on bicycle and climate action plans, zero waste, agricultural inventory, green areas and activities on important anniversaries of the founding of the Republic, starting with the 100th anniversary of Atatürk's arrival in Ankara, and these decisions were unanimously approved by the Greater Ankara Municipality Assembly.

Core Concepts of Ankara Citizen Council

Because there was no effective citizen council in the capital Ankara before, Ankara Citizen Council's components proceeded with a participation strategy aiming to ensure that the concept of a citizen council is understood and adopted in the city. To this end, the components adopted effective facilitation approaches in organizing and developed a different understanding by drawing lessons from the general experience of citizen councils in Türkiye. Although this approach was not fully understood by the civil society elements in the city at first, the successes achieved over time have shown that these methods work. The following basic principles were adopted in the implementation of the citizen council in Ankara:

Openness and transparency

Ankara Citizen council considers the principles of openness and transparency as an inherent objective in all its actions and transactions and acts accordingly. In this respect, it reflects its decisions to the public openly and transparently and carries out its activities in this way.

Accountability

Ankara Citizen council carries out all its activities in an accountable manner to the society and its constituents. In this structure, which is organized as a General Assembly, chairperson, executive board, assemblies and working groups, all units supervise each other thanks to the horizontal organization model.

Transversality

Ankara Citizen council components are involved at all scales, from the neighborhood level to the city level. Thus, the network and opportunity for communication between scales and jointly developing solutions to urban problems are expanding.

Awareness for citizen councils

As the council of the capital city, Ankara Citizen council has raised awareness of citizen councils across Türkiye. As it set an example, citizen councils started to be established in other cities one after the other. This awareness has been achieved through various activities and projects.

Interaction with Stakeholders

Stakeholders of Ankara Citizen Council become a part of this culture when they participate in the work and meetings of the council and contribute to the development of the city by developing an interaction network within the council. Thanks to this interaction network, a common mind is established within the city and stakeholders serve the city in a pluralistic order with the power arising from unity.

Interaction among stakeholders

As an institution, Ankara Citizen Council supports the work of its stakeholders on behalf of the city and develops an effective and efficient communication process with stakeholders. With this communication process, a democratic mechanism and the implementation of governance principles are ensured.

Visibility

Ankara Citizen Council is visible both in physical parts of the city and on social media to consider citizens' suggestions regarding the city. Activities and projects are carried out to realize this.

Widespread Impact

The activities carried out by Ankara Citizen Council on behalf of the city and its advisory role to the Greater Ankara Municipality have an impact on the entire city and society as a whole. Therefore, the activities and projects realized are both unique in terms of quality and applicable to the entire city.

Institutionalization

Despite the short period since its establishment, Ankara Citizen Council has played a major role in establishing Ankara's values within the society and in the branding of the city. It has achieved this both by organizing the working groups and assemblies in its organization per its purpose and by incorporating Ankara's values into its structure. Thus, Ankara has gained an institutionalized and established citizen council.

Social benefit

Ankara Citizen council works to realize social benefit in all its actions and transactions. To ensure the urban development of Ankara and the protection of its historical and cultural heritage, a common ground is reached with all Ankara residents, and the benefit of the entire city is prioritized with the principle of social benefit.

Innovation

Ankara Citizen council supports innovative ideas and initiatives. In this way, it hosts professionals with qualifications in various professions who can advise the young and entrepreneurial individuals of the city. In this way, young and entrepreneurial youth are encouraged, and the values of the city are supported within the city.

Neutrality

Ankara Citizen council has adopted the principle of impartiality in all its actions, works and transactions. Thus, it exhibits a supra-ideological approach and generates solutions to problems by prioritizing the interests of the city as a whole.

Result-oriented working

Ankara Citizen council strives to find solutions to the problems of citizens living in the city. It also works to turn Ankara into a cultural, historical and artistic capital and to solve the problems that arise in this process. The Council cooperates with other institutions and organizations to carry out activities that are considered to be beneficial for society and takes initiatives by preserving its core values in order to achieve results.

Management Structure of Ankara Citizen Council

A closer look at the legislation on citizen councils reveals two main problems in terms of organization especially based on the experience of Ankara Citizen Council. The first of these problems can be seen in the relationship between the chairperson and executive boards elected in the general assembly, where all citizen council members come together, and the working groups and assemblies of the citizen council, which are formed voluntarily. Since the citizen council is a purely voluntary structure, it can be difficult to spread the understanding that elected bodies have no sanctions on voluntary structures and that there should not be a hierarchy, even though these details are not provided in the legislation. As a result, sometimes citizen council presidents and executive boards try to implement a hierarchical management approach that is not activated to them, while sometimes working groups and assemblies try to create their spheres of power outside the integrity of the citizen council. In both cases, the growth of voluntary unity in terms of participation is interrupted or even shrunk, and citizen councils cannot be effective in their cities. As a result, the ability of citizen councils, which are formed through a representative formation process, to organize widespread participation by controlling the power field that emerges as a natural consequence of this representation committee can only be possible through a culture and practice of participation in which the behavioral patterns of the participants are constantly redefined and flexibly defined. Each citizen council must constantly discuss, keep on the agenda and negotiate the foundations of the culture of participation and the behavioral patterns of the council's components in its own specific and specific context. Only in this way can a citizen council transform its potential into a participatory dynamic and create impact. Undoubtedly, such an endeavor is not easy and requires a challenging and emotionally charged self-criticism and capacity for self-change, starting from the individual, and extending to groups, council components and the citizen council itself.

The second main problem is how the organizational form introduced by the legislation for citizen councils will be implemented in different local government units. Naturally, the components of the general assembly of citizen councils will differ according to the social structure, size and scale of the city in which they are located. However, the legislation on citizen councils does not take this differentiation into account. According to the legislation, all municipalities, whether metropolitan or non-metropolitan, town, district or provincial, follow the same organizational approach. Especially in the case of metropolitan cities, this creates serious problems. Some of the problems stem from the large number of institutions and organizations that have the right to be members of the citizen council, while others stem from the complex network of relationships that arise due to the large number of local government units and public institutions. There has not yet been a systematic structure on how participation will be organized within the gradation starting from mukhtars and neighborhood associations at the neighborhood level to district municipalities, and from district municipalities to citizen councils and metropolitan municipal councils. There are also serious problems in the harmonization between the methods of election and participation. Especially in Ankara, Istanbul and Izmir, cities with populations approaching 25 million, it is therefore very difficult to determine how the communication and participation activities carried out by the local governments themselves and the dynamics in the field of civil society will work together with the citizen council. For this reason, in practice, each citizen council tries to find its way in the face of these two problems and strives to develop its methods.

Undoubtedly, these problems have been known and widely discussed all over Türkiye since 2005, when citizen councils were introduced into municipal legislation. For this reason, Ankara Citizen Council adopted an innovative organizational approach when it was first established by evaluating past experiences, especially in determining the position of the executive board and the chairperson. In this approach, the principles of avoiding political tension with the current local administration, establishing a relationship with the bureaucratic structure of the municipality on the basis of urban policies, and ensuring that all citizens, institutions and organizations in the city can freely take part in the citizen council, creating a truly horizontal organizational structure and preventing the formation of areas of power belonging to individuals or groups in any part of the citizen council within the framework of existing habits were important. It can be said that the most important structure in putting these principles into practice is the executive committee. Work started with an executive board with a high representation power at the scale of Ankara province. In this context, it is important to have a representative from each of the political parties with a group in the Greater Ankara Municipality Assembly on the executive board and to ensure that key stakeholders such as academia, trade unions, professional chambers and mukhtars are represented in the executive board on a gender basis. However, what is even more important than these categories are that the citizen council president and the executive board adopt a secretariat role to facilitate the policy-making processes of working groups and assemblies at lower levels of participatory organization. To this end, the president and executive board members of the citizen council have frequently stated publicly that they have adopted this approach and have carried out their decision-making processes in this way.

In practice, all proposals for projects, policies and approaches that come from working groups and assemblies, or that somehow reach the executive board, are tried to be considered in the words of all working groups and assemblies as far as possible. The principle has been adopted that proposals coming directly from working groups and assemblies are presented and discussed by spokespersons to the Steering Committee. In addition, in all the work carried out, it is important to ensure the visibility of all stakeholders involved in the process and to create motivation. In this way, it was possible to define the citizen council not as a hierarchical decision-making mechanism, but as a field of action in which active citizens are responsible for the activities carried out to realize the policy alternatives produced in the face of urban problems. Closely related to this is the approach that the working methods, directives and production methods of working groups and assemblies are in no way determined and directed by the chairperson and the executive committee. Although there were sometimes debates about who should exercise decision-making power in practice as a result of this approach, at the end of the day it was understood that the citizen council was not and could not be an area of power and that the determined actions could only be strengthened within the framework of mutual tolerance and understanding, and to a certain extent this has turned into a culture. The most important consequence of this situation was the widespread perception that there is no hierarchy in a truly horizontal organization, that the election of organs such as the chairperson and the executive committee is merely a change of flag, and that the condition for such organs to exercise power can only be legitimized on the grounds of supporting participatory practices. As a result, although the coming together of a significant number of institutions and organizations in a large participatory organization such as Ankara Citizen Council is seen as a space of power, both the existence and sustainability of this space depend on the values it is based on and the districts it embraces. In practice, such an understanding has reduced the instrumentality of potentially tense processes such as general assemblies and election processes and has enabled it to distance itself from everyday politics.

The first executive board of Ankara Citizen Council in 2019 consisted of 23 members. Over time, each of these executive board members adopted these values and tried to contribute to the participatory process. The fact that very few executive board members were mentioned in the communication processes reflected to the public in the 4-year experience of the council, while the names of many working group and assembly spokespersons and volunteers were mentioned can be considered as a result of this. In fact, the rapid growth of the citizen council, the increase in the number of its members and the spread of its activities are closely related to this culture. Undoubtedly, from time to time, there have been participants who have sensed the social power potential created by the citizen council and wanted to use it for various purposes. In such cases, the basic principle within the citizen council is that the citizen council cannot be used to create a sphere of power and that the source of legitimacy is the participatory communication and partnership bond established with others and the efforts and production made within the citizen council. There is also a tradition of addressing the organizational process of citizen councils through discussions on the structure and composition of general assemblies and how the election process will take place. In the past, in citizen councils established in various parts of Türkiye, there have been discussions on setting quotas for elections and evaluating list and sheet election procedures. However, most of these discussions have reduced the functioning of citizen councils to the level of an ordinary civil society organization or local government assembly, rather than deepening the understanding of participation in the citizen council. In the ordinary period between general assemblies, there are very few discussions on how citizen councils should function. Problematic situations and tensions are mostly related to the directives and related processes that will determine the elections of citizen councils. This inevitable vicious circle has resulted in citizen councils increasingly being perceived as a sphere of power with its resources rather than a participatory structure. This is perhaps the biggest challenge for citizen councils in Türkiye, which Ankara Citizen Council has been openly trying to avoid since its establishment.

After the 2021 General Assembly, it was aimed to increase inclusiveness by expanding the senior management. The creation of a 35-member executive board, a 40-member advisory board and a board of honor initially created confusion in working groups and assemblies, but over time, it was seen that the main units in practice were the working groups and assemblies at the grassroots level and the functionality of these boards was ensured. It was thought that the advisory board would convene once a year as a custom, the executive board would convene every 3 months with an executive structure, and the board of honor would convene once during its term of office. With this structure, the functionality of a citizen council with 1800 members and nearly 5,000 volunteers has been ensured in a large metropolis like the capital Ankara.

Working groups and assemblies

The concept of politics points to a very important distinction for city councils. City councils do not deal with the concept of "politics", which refers to current and daily power struggles, but with "politics", which refers to an attitude and approach that expresses the general orientation in any field or issue. Policy debate is a long-term, multi-actor and content-based discussion. Undoubtedly, policy debates can also have political repercussions. However, just as it is wrong to call city councils completely non-political structures, it is equally wrong to see city councils as a part of current politics other than policy making. As a result, city councils contribute to the development of the space for the action of local politics by addressing alternative policies that can provide solutions to the problem areas where politics discuss the results through participatory methods.

As a requirement of the legislation on citizen councils and the spirit of participatory democracy, working groups and assemblies have emerged as the kitchens of citizen councils or as centers for the production of ideas and participatory culture. It can be said that assemblies and working groups were defined in Türkiye by drawing on the previous Local Agenda 21 experience and different participatory approaches at the local level. However, it cannot be said that there has been much clarification in terms of defining working groups and assemblies and establishing their practices in the fifteen years since the legislation on citizen councils was drafted. Nevertheless, it is observed that in different regions of Türkiye, assemblies and working groups formed under citizen councils have emerged with some characteristics reflecting local dynamics. For example, in Thrace, working groups and assemblies have an important place in environmental struggles; in Çanakkale, for example, there are important experiences in planning and participatory budgeting; in Istanbul, the Aegean and Mediterranean regions, gender and cultural differences come to the fore; and the experiences of working groups and assemblies differ in almost every settlement. This differentiation may be influenced by factors such as how local problems will be addressed by citizen councils and municipalities, the existing culture of participation, local knowledge on the issues to be addressed, and the role of civil society elements in the citizen council.

In cities such as Ankara, where there has not been a sustainable citizen council experience before, citizen councils are not recognized and how working groups and assemblies will be formed and contribute to different thematic and urban problem areas is an important problem area. The lack of knowledge and experience on issues such as the formation of working groups on which subjects and the formation processes of assemblies necessitate innovations in line with the principles of participatory processes and monitoring the results. In Ankara Citizen Council, a similar process was followed in the formation of working groups and assemblies. From the first general assembly onwards, an approach based on the participation and feedback of council members in the formation of assemblies and working groups was tried to be followed. This was because, after a twenty-five-year period of local political polarization and conflict, it was foreseen that if the structures to be established in the capital city of Ankara, which has serious deficiencies in terms of participatory behavior, collective action, co-thinking and co-production practices, were established as a direct extension of the existing political and bureaucratic apparatus, the citizen council would enter a process of working or not working in a way that would not be in line with its founding principles.

In particular, the elected president and executive board of the citizen council had significant reservations on these issues. For this reason, member participation was taken as a basis in the formation of the working groups of the citizen council and contribution to urban processes in the formation of the assemblies. For this purpose, starting from the first general assembly, the opinions of the citizen council members on which assemblies and working groups should be established were taken, and processes were carried out by collecting their opinions on which of these they would like to take part in through prepared forms.

After the first general assembly of Ankara Citizen Council on June 29, 2019, intensive negotiations were held primarily for women's and youth assemblies. The formation of these two assemblies, whose names are listed separately in the legislation on citizen councils, was considered important. However, it was observed that the civil society elements interested in these two assemblies were mainly interested in the possible political and institutional effects of these structures to be established at the scale of Ankara, rather than the concepts of women and youth in their themes, it was decided to leave the establishment process of these two assemblies to time, considering that there was a need for a learning process in this regard. The aim was for Ankara to grasp the concept of citizen councils first, and then to establish these two important councils. As a matter of fact, after three years, with the increased awareness of the meaning of the citizen council concept, it was thought that the necessary steps could now be taken for the establishment of women's and youth assemblies. The definitions made in the directive approved unanimously at the 3rd General Assembly held on February 29, 2020, were also considered to contribute to this. However, this could not be realized due to the difficulties created by the Covid-19 Pandemic process and the problems encountered in the execution of existing working groups and assemblies on the scale of Ankara province. As an instructive start for these processes, a youth assembly working group was formed at the end of 2020 for the formation of an inclusive and participatory youth assembly, and this working group was transformed into an assembly by holding its general assembly at the beginning of 2022 after about a year and a half of work. In the event of similar conditions, it is aimed to initiate work for a women's assembly.

Interestingly, the open-door approach of Ankara Citizen Council, which accepts all applicants from civil society, has led to a different approach for the councils. There are two important examples in this regard. The first example is the Bicycle Assembly. The members of ABIDOSD (Ankara Cyclists and Nature Sports Association), which was formed by bicycle associations and university bicycle clubs in Ankara that came together simultaneously with the establishment of Ankara Citizen Council, attracted attention with their contributions to the bicycle-related projects and practices of the Greater Ankara Municipality and the establishment of the Citizen council. This sincere effort paved the way for the Executive Board of Ankara Citizen Council to propose to the Association and its components to establish a bicycle council under the roof of the citizen council. As a result, with a decision officially approved by the general assembly, the "Bicycle Council" was established, perhaps the first of its kind in Türkiye. After its establishment, the bicycle assembly determined its own directive, members and working principles, formed working groups and started to effectively monitor developments in the field of bicycling in Ankara. The second example is the Castle Studies Council. After its establishment, Ankara Citizen Council organized a large meeting at Ankara Castle with the participation of artisans, academics, tourists, local government representatives and the public. This community of about one hundred and forty members, which has been coming together for many years with the contributions of some politicians and has been working on the Castle, has also accepted to become an assembly of Ankara Citizen Council. Ankara Castle Studies Assembly can be called a first in this sense. This council makes important contributions in monitoring the works in the historical texture and highlighting the historical texture with social and cultural activities.

In four years, the "Assembly of Disabled Citizens" was the first assembly formed by Ankara Citizen Council with the participation of all its members at all stages. The establishment process of the Assembly of Disabled Citizens was in a sense defined as a learning process for the citizen council. For this purpose, a stakeholder analysis was conducted with those who expressed interest among the members of the citizen council and representatives of registered non-governmental organizations in Ankara specializing in disabled people. A coordination structure was established to organize the first general assembly of the Assembly of Disabled Citizens, which was completed with approximately two hundred participants. In the general assembly, planning was made by considering the needs of different disabled groups, and as a result, a coordination board was established to fulfill the processes of the Assembly of Disabled Citizens. They forwarded important recommendations on disability to the Third General Assembly. Then, in the fall of 2021, the general assembly of the Assembly of Disabled Citizens was held, and the president and executive board were elected. The Assembly of Disabled Citizens has reached a working maturity that reflects this institutional experience.

As the citizen council experience entered its fourth year, the other two councils established were the youth council and the environment and climate council. The youth assembly first started meeting in 2020 with an incubator mentality and a working group mentality, then gradually grew and became one of the largest youth assemblies in Türkiye by 2023. Especially after the major earthquake disaster in Türkiye in 2023, the youth assembly showed that it was an exemplary structure with the solidarity process it initiated. The environment and climate council was formed by the merger of the environmental working groups under the roof of the citizen council. Especially in a period when the effects of climate change on Anatolia have become visible, it has been making important contributions by working on issues such as the right to water and climate action planning.

An innovative approach was also followed in the formation of working groups. First, at the 2nd General Assembly held on October 5, 2019, forms were distributed to all members regarding which working groups they would like to take part in, and their preferences were taken. The importance of each member contributing to the working groups as much as possible was conveyed. As a result of the planning efforts, all 17 working groups held their first meeting simultaneously on a weekend in December 2019. At this first meeting, the working groups were asked to elect a spokesperson, identify experts and other CSOs to be invited to the group, and determine the date of the next meeting. A significant number of the working groups started their work in this way and continue to work successfully. One of the working groups, "Architecture

Culture and Planning", is composed of academics from the faculties of architecture in 21 universities in Ankara and became a working group because of the meetings with the citizen council. As the citizen council completes its fourth year, there are nearly thirty working groups, including those that have been decided to be established. Approximately 5,000 volunteers involved in these working groups also act together with the citizen council.

In the work of the working groups and assemblies so far, efforts have been made to work on communication, learning and capacity building in terms of the participatory thought generation process. Work has been done on framing an issue related to urban problems, interacting with the right stakeholders, how to increase interaction within and outside the working group, and the quality of the final products. So far, the working groups have done important work on many issues such as the promotion of the citizen council, organizing solidarity during the Covid-19 Pandemic, developing strategies for the protection of historical sites, the right to water and urban infrastructure, and nurturing hope in this area.

Naturally, there are also various problems in the functioning of working groups. While some working groups are very active, others do not seem to be able to make progress. There may be various reasons for this. Issues such as concerns about doing work outside of the subject, excessive or insufficient interest, and difficulties in operating in the field of study can create performance differences between working groups. For this reason, the Executive Board of the Citizen council often tries to establish close relations with the spokespersons of working groups and assemblies and tries to standardize their work performance within a partnership culture. As a result, it can be said that what is desired has been achieved and a working group and assembly-oriented working style has been established in the citizen council. Although this book will not be able to cover each structure separately, the following chapters will include the contributions of specific studies on the subject.

List of assemblies

3. Bicycle Assembly
4. Ankara Castle Works Assembly
5. People with Disabilities Assembly
6. Capital City Youth Assembly
7. Environment and Climate Assembly

List of working Groups

1. Research for the city of Ankara
2. Funds and projects
3. Hacı Bayram-ı Veli and cultural interaction
4. Public health and addiction
5. Animal rights
6. Urban aesthetics
7. Rural development
8. Culture and art
9. Architecture culture and planning
10. Industry and trade
11. Sports
12. Technology
13. Tourism promotion
14. Consumer rights
15. Education
16. Social innovation
17. Brand city Ankara
18. Children of the capital

19. Neighborhood culture
20. 100th anniversary
21. Media
22. Disaster management
23. Migration

With these principles and this organizational structure, Ankara Citizen Council represents a very interesting experience in Türkiye's political and democratic life. This experience has been followed with interest and taken as a reference by other citizen councils in Türkiye for some time. The work done has gone far beyond the definition of a citizen council and has led to a pioneering role in organizing solidarity both during the Covid-19 Pandemic and in many other disasters in Türkiye. In addition, bringing together the stakeholders of the city of Ankara on one platform paved the way for the discussion of many policy options for the city and the emergence of a new culture of participation. These results have enabled the citizen council to be recognized internationally, with two important international awards recognizing the council's experience. In the following sections of this book, these achievements will be discussed under specific headings.

Reference

Şahin, S. Z. (2011) 'An evaluation on the contributions of city councils to participatory urban governance: The case of Ankara', City Councils Symposium Proceedings.

4. Activities and Achievements of Ankara Citizen Council

Formation of Institutional Relationships

As mentioned earlier, citizen councils have a different outlook than other institutional structures in a country like Türkiye, which is centralized and has strong bureaucratic traditions. The fact that they do not have a legal personality but are official structures defined in the municipal law gives citizen councils a stronger legitimacy than other NGOs and platforms. This legitimacy is further strengthened by the fact that the constituent elements of this structure are primarily representatives of civil society organizations, professional associations, and public institutions, with legal personality, and with representatives who can act independently of the boundaries of the existing institutional culture. In this way, ordinary citizens can relate to this structure. However, this legitimacy is also very fragile. When the institutional reflexes and cultures of the constituents of the citizen council become dominant, and when situations arise against development and expansion, the space for legitimacy narrows down and citizen councils become stunted and weak. Many citizen councils in Türkiye are in this situation. To prevent this situation, it is necessary to keep open the channels of dialogue, diplomacy, conflict resolution, contact, and interaction based on open communication transparency and active implementation of the values shared by the individuals who make up the citizen councils.

These important dimensions need to be considered in the development of institutional relations. Since its establishment, Ankara Citizen Council has tried to move forward with an awareness of the importance of participation. First, unlike other institutional structures, it does not make a distinction between internal and external stakeholders in citizen councils. This is because the organizational structure of the citizen council functions entirely as a network of stakeholders. The geographical location of the stakeholders is the only factor in the separation of stakeholders. To draw a certain boundary in the conduct of participatory processes, each citizen council is considered subject to the boundaries of the local governments in which it is established. On the other hand, since all civil society components and citizens participating in citizen councils are united in a non-action-oriented policy-making process, the main purpose of all activities is to exchange views and ensure interaction. This unprecedented point of view, the set of institutional relations that take place in and around citizen councils, brings the concept of citizen councils into question. Trying to answer questions such as what the definition of citizen councils is, what they can do, and why they should do it commonly is realized together with the activities of citizen councils. Although sometimes a tiring endeavor, such an approach and experience allow for very fruitful discussions on participation.

It can be said that there are two important areas of activity in the formation of institutional relations. The first is the representational activities of the president and executive board of the citizen council, and the second is the negotiations between the civic elements of the citizen council and external actors. For the legitimacy provided to citizen councils by the legislation to become visible, the elected chairperson and executive board need to make some contacts and visits, accept visits in return, and gain institutional visibility. However, this visibility needs to be directly related to the founding objectives of the citizen councils. Otherwise, relationships that are supposed to reinforce legitimacy may have the opposite effect. In many cases, problems of trust may arise when the reasons why citizen councils make such visits are not fully explained to the public or when no tangible output is achieved because of the visits. There may even be conflicts with the political sphere of influence of elected mayors and local councilors. One of the main ways in which this can be prevented is for structures such as working groups based on volunteering to carry out these activities instead of elected bodies such as the chairperson and the executive board of the citizen council. For this purpose, it is important that volunteers who take part in the working groups and assemblies of citizen councils and determine their working methods interact among themselves, with other working groups and institutions, and with the relevant units of the municipality. Undoubtedly, such activities of the elected and voluntary bodies of the citizen council must be carried out in a certain coordination with each other, and inevitably, after a certain point, such cross-relationships and intersections will increase. In certain cases, it is important that the president and the executive board of the citizen council, as the top decision-making body, take part in the establishment of institutional relations where the influence of working groups and assemblies may not be sufficient.

Within the framework of this approach, Ankara Citizen Council has tried to develop certain institutional relations, acting in line with the mission of being in the capital city of Türkiye, Ankara. First and foremost, good relations with the Mayor of Greater Ankara Municipality, members of the Greater Ankara Municipality Assembly, bureaucrats, and administrators of Ankara Municipality have been developed. In addition, regular goodwill meetings were held with the Governorship of Ankara, which has a legal representative in the Citizen Council. Once these relations at the local level were firmly established, all institutions and organizations associated with citizen councils at the central government level were contacted. Among these, the General Directorate of Local Governments under the Ministry of Environment, Urbanization, and Climate Change, to which citizen councils are institutionally affiliated, is the most prominent. A close contact was also established with the Ministry of Culture and Tourism concerning sustainable development and urban culture. Since it was the first time that a citizen council of this scale and effectiveness was established in the capital Ankara for citizen participation, meetings were also held at the international level. Direct contact was made with the EU Delegation to Türkiye, the French Embassy, and, where appropriate, with the United Nations Development Program. However, the main purpose of all these meetings was to introduce the concept of a citizen council and to express the benefits that a well-functioning citizen council could bring to Ankara and Türkiye. The emergence of a perception of a citizen council that tries to replace elected and appointed officials was seen as a problem area and tried to be avoided at the beginning.

Besides, Ankara Citizen Council also had direct contacts and joint meetings with the Çankaya, Yenimahalle, Etimesgut, and Polatlı Citizen Councils established at the district level in the same city. Although the legislation does not define any hierarchical or similar relationship between metropolitan and district citizen councils, efforts were made to establish a relationship of equals with these citizen councils. On the other hand, high-level meetings were held with the Union of Citizen Councils of Türkiye and the Platform of Citizen Councils of Türkiye, two unofficial umbrella organizations in Türkiye. As a result of these meetings, Ankara Citizen Council became a member of both supreme unions. In addition, the "Metropolitan Citizen Councils Initiative" was launched with the initiative of Ankara Citizen Council for metropolitan citizen councils to share experiences among themselves. Over time, relations with the Union of Citizen Councils of Türkiye have progressed more rapidly and in 2023, Ankara Citizen Council assumed the presidency of the Union on the occasion of the 100th anniversary of the Republic. In addition, Ankara Citizen Council, with the mission of being located in the capital city of Ankara, has also contacted political parties and central governmental organizations working on similar issues to explain the meaning and importance of citizen councils. These include the Union of Municipalities of Türkiye and the Ombudsman's Office.

Working groups and assemblies established outside the senior management of the Citizen Council have also been in constant contact with other working groups and assemblies within the council and with different institutional structures. Over time, a certain level of coordination has been established between the meetings of the senior management of the Citizen council and its sub-organizations. This has enabled continuity and sustainability in the issues of interest and focus. The principle of conducting all kinds of institutional relations within a common framework based on the principle of showing interest in the subject matter, without any distinction of institutional authority, has been realized. Depending on the purpose, outcome, and output of the relations, the formation of the institutional structure and the development of institutional relations could be carried out simultaneously. Sometimes the formation of a working group and the implementation of certain activities were carried out at the same time as a form of mediation with other relevant units and institutions. This approach often enabled the growth and expansion of the citizen council and institutionalization to take place together. In this respect, it can be said that this is one of the important specificities of Ankara Citizen Council. Although this uniqueness sometimes leads the citizen council and its components to activities with specific outputs by taking them out of policy-making activities, it can be claimed that policy processes have also become more effective in this way.

However, this unique aspect also posed certain challenges for a civic platform. First of all, this flexible learning approach has facilitated bringing various issues to the agenda with a speed that is exciting for the volunteers of the citizen council. However, problems arose because many of the institutions with which the citizen council engaged did not have this flexibility and agility. For example, the municipality and its departments were sometimes unable to respond to the sheer volume of requests from the citizen council and the scale of the citizen council's activities, and bureaucratic power-grabbing reflexes were activated. As mentioned earlier, local governments are not resilient administrations in many countries, including Türkiye. Municipal council members or local organization members of political parties who are involved in politics in the municipality may be under the misconception that the citizen council may have a certain political agenda. This resulted in an increased perception of threat from the citizen council and negatively affected the institutionalization process. On the contrary, it has also been witnessed that volunteer members of citizen councils have tried to create a of power for themselves. As a result, certain power conflicts may occur over the question of how to use the resources and opportunities provided by the municipality to the citizen council, even if limited. In response to the question of how all this can be reconciled; various institutionalization approaches have been tried to be implemented. Past examples show that in some cases, citizen councils have tried to determine the functioning of the citizen councils by setting rules and putting them into effect in the form of directives. In other cases, solutions based on the initiatives of leaders have been implemented. Clarke (2017) points out differences between state-centric and society-centric models that affect local governance, both of which have some advantages in a collaborative decision-making process. In both cases, certain problems arise. Since directives are not binding, citizen councils become overly bureaucratized or unwieldy. On the other hand, institutional solutions that are dependent on individuals undermine the civic shared character of citizen councils.

Another critical point is that governance is not synonymous with good governance, which requires core institutional values (Hendrik, 2014). This difference also invites a discussion on the organizational characteristics of local governments that are imperative for good governance at a more operational level (Bolton & Leach, 2002). In the end, it can be claimed that each citizen council has a unique experience of institutionalization under the determination of all these opportunities and obstacles. While in some, rules and written principles are more important, in others an understanding based on ritualistic and ceremonial habits based on institutional culture, space, and social relations may be more effective, which is an indication of a resilient governance approach Recently, social media and alternative communication channels have also contributed to institutionalization. In the case of Ankara Citizen Council, an institutionalization process based on practical learning of common principles, which highlights the visibility of volunteer labor in social media and communication channels, seems to be effective. Although there have been conflicts in this process with components with institutionalist or sanctioning tendencies based on previous civil society experiences, as a result of the experience since 2019, Ankara Citizen Council has been able to develop some institutional reflexes that determine which problems in the city, how, in what form and at what level to intervene. However, given that Türkiye is going through difficult political processes, it may not be possible to develop an approach to every problem in the city.

When the experience of Ankara Citizen Council is evaluated from an institutional perspective, it can be said that it has a positive rather than a reactive approach. In the past two decades, the city of Ankara was governed by a mayor who was largely anti-participatory. This has led to a predominantly reactionary approach by civil society components in the city against projects and policies that they perceived as negative. Particularly, professional chambers and neighborhood associations organized protests and filed lawsuits against municipal policies that were almost criminal against Ankara's heritage. Over time, this approach gradually turned into a cautious behavior. When the mayor changed and a participatory structure such as Ankara Citizen Council was established, it was not easy for civil society organizations in the city to adapt to this structure. On the other hand, although local governments often state that they advocate participation in principle, in practice they are often weak in explaining and negotiating their own or other public institutions' projects through a participatory process. Therefore, while some actors in the city were pushing the citizen council to pursue a similar mission, those who had never been involved in participation processes in the city were expecting more positive approaches. For this reason, Ankara Citizen Council was formed with a structure that preferred to carry out the institutionalization process with more affirmative and proactive approaches. This is also because many citizen segments whose problems and solution proposals regarding the city have not been taken into consideration so far have found a place in the citizen council. At this point, it can be said that Ankara Citizen Council has adopted an approach that combines institutionalization with institutional relations, minimizes struggles prone to failure and disappointment, and circulates solution-oriented approaches to the city. At the root of this approach is the effort to maximize the interaction of a network of actors and institutions that draws its richness from its diversity.

Advisory decision mechanism

According to the legislation in force in Türkiye, the most important domain of citizen councils is to formulate recommendations. Accordingly, when a citizen council's working groups and assemblies develop various recommendations for the city, they are sent to the municipal council and must be included in the agenda of the first meeting of the municipal council. Given that the mayor has the authority to set the agenda of the municipal council according to the current municipal law in Türkiye, this can be seen as almost equivalent to the authority granted to the mayor. However, it is unclear how these recommendations will be handled, what the sanctions will be, and how and by whom the implementation will be monitored if the recommendations are approved by the municipal council. Nevertheless, the possibility of getting a recommendation on the agenda of the municipal council is an important source of motivation for those active in citizen councils. In this sense, it can be said that these recommendations are the most important part of local policy-making processes. However, how to formulate recommendations, their content, scope, format, and many other issues need to be conveyed to the volunteers in a participatory process in the citizen council followed by a learning process needs to take place. Otherwise, recommendations that are far from realistic or that are not feasible because they are beyond the limits of authority may emerge. For this reason, it can be said that the process of institutionalization of the citizen council should be sustained simultaneously during the formulation of recommendations.

Therefore, immediately after the formation of the working groups and assemblies of Ankara Citizen Council, training and awareness-raising activities were carried out regularly. The aim of these activities was to share the work of different working groups and assemblies and to ensure coordination within the citizen council organization. The objectives and working principles of the citizen councils were the primary issues addressed in these meetings. It was reminded that there are international documents, principles, and concepts that should be kept in mind in the work of the citizen council as required by the legislation, and it was conveyed that it is imperative to refer to them although the citizen council seems to be a structure, which is more independent. It was explained that there may be activities outside of the scope of sustainable development, citizens' law, urban rights, transparency, and accountability in governance, but ultimately it is important to relate to these concepts. Since it may not be easy for everyone to learn and keep track of these documents, principles, and concepts, the first activity report of Ankara Citizen Council published in 2020 was designed to include information on these issues.

Among the issues that determine the working principles of citizen councils, the concepts of common urban consciousness, common knowledge of urban history, common behavioral patterns, common understanding of the quality of life, tolerance, respect, a common sense of responsibility, and public thinking were conveyed in terms of citizenship law; basic human rights, labor, and related rights, solidarity rights (urban rights), the right to the city. Rights seeking and advocacy and the legal framework related to rights were emphasized in terms of urban rights; transparency, accountability, openness, participation in terms of good governance, effectiveness/efficiency, the governance cycle, and strategic management. In discussing these concepts, there are some fundamental issues that council volunteers need to be aware of, which are based on discussions within the council. One of the most important issues is the conditions for harnessing the power of citizen councils, which lack a budget, executive authority, and legal personality. In this respect, the need to pay attention to institutional boundaries and the distinction between representation and participation in citizen council work, as well as the need to be aware of local policies and strategies. This is because it is important to be aware that proposals made without sufficient knowledge of the work of local government units will not have a serious impact. The importance of horizontal organization and participation starts from the neighborhood level, without forgetting that the issues of interest have bureaucratic counterparts. In this sense, it is stated that the activities of the citizen council bodies better involve the following content:

- Discussing urban problems,
- Conducting studies on urban policies,
- Contributing to public awareness-raising in the city,
- Contributing to the participatory and accountable functioning of local government,
- Conducting studies on belonging and urban identity,
- Contributing to the self-expression of interest groups in the city,

- Conducting studies on urban rights.

The ultimate aim of these activities is to produce recommendations to be considered by the local government. When a recommendation is to be made on any urban issue, some preliminary work needs to be done. Existing studies on the subject to be recommended, whether the recommendations have the qualities of impartiality, independence, and publicity, whether interviews and consultations have been held with the authorities, experts, and institutional agencies responsible or have the authority with the subject in concern while formulating the recommendations, and the creation of a common ground regarding the recommendations. To this end, examples from Türkiye and the world were frequently explained and advised to working groups and councils. The recommendations approved by the Executive Board are sent to the Department of Official Documents and Decisions of the Municipality to be forwarded to the Greater Ankara Municipality Assembly. Once the relevant recommendation is approved, the only task of the citizen council is to ask and follow up on the fate of the decision. Yet, usually, the citizen council can not intervene in work procedures and expenditures in the activities for the execution of the decision. There may be projects where every detail has been negotiated with the citizen council and municipal units at every stage, but it is necessary to be patient and keep expectations low since the legislation gave an advisory position to the citizen councils without any reference to the execution process. There may be projects that are not accepted or cannot be realized. The responsibility for this lies with the municipality. These principles are discussed openly and regularly, and a meaningful balance is sought in the relations between the citizen council, its components, working groups and assemblies, and the municipality.

It is also frequently explained that the activities of working groups and assemblies are subject to the same principles as those of the executive and the chairperson, which working groups and assemblies are structures open to participation and dialogue, that they are secretariats, and that they cannot operate as closed, bureaucratic power centers. The Council Directive, which was accepted by the General Assembly of Ankara Citizen Council in 2020, sets out the basic principles regarding the internal organs of the Council. Working groups meet at least once every three (3) months and submit a report on their work to the Executive Board once every six (6) months. The activities of working groups that do not comply with these conditions may be terminated with the decision of the absolute majority of the Executive Board. Working groups are established with the acceptance by the Executive Board of the application of at least five (5) members or specialized institutions or organizations on the subject of the working group. Working groups and assemblies can send their advisory decision proposals to the Executive Boars including the activity, purpose, goal, scope, project team, parties, principles and methods, work plan and program proposals related to their subject matter. Working groups shall submit a work plan to the Executive Board within two (2) months at the latest after their establishment, including working group activities and stakeholders.

Ankara Citizen Council has also tried to develop an approach to advocacy, as one of its most important activities. Accordingly, the principles developed together with working groups and assemblies are as follows:

- City council advocacy activities should follow a sequence of information, dialogue, and negotiation.
- Advocacy-related activities, statements, lawsuits, press releases, and actions of city council components cannot be publicly expressed by the citizen council executive or chairperson without being discussed directly within the citizen council.
- The right approach to advocacy in city councils should be the activism of constituents and the dialogue and negotiation of the citizen council administration.

Some issues of day-to-day functioning are also dealt with in working groups and assemblies. To this end, the following principles have been developed:

- No organ of the city council is or will be bureaucratic.
- In communication between Council bodies, face-to-face, video, and audio, and if not possible, written communication should be used as much as possible, except for official correspondence.
- It should be kept in mind that discussions and communication are not productive in channels open to the other components of city councils and the public and the framework of communication is important.
- It should not be forgotten that Ankara Citizen Council covers 6 million Ankara residents and all provincial borders.
- It is ineffective for working groups and assemblies to become closed and shrinking groups. The first task of working groups and assemblies is to improve their quality and quantity regarding a dynamic structure.
- In any case, there is no subordinate-superior relationship between the bodies, including the secretariat, except for specialized knowledge.
- The main work of the city council is to work on urban public policy-making in line with its objectives.
- These studies may also include elements for execution, but the most prioritized issue is to carry

out studies that will create a consensus on certain themes.

- Workshops, awareness-raising activities, research, and all kinds of activities to develop proposals are the priority activities of the council.
- After a certain period, the quality of the documents that the council and its bodies will produce on all activities such as recommendations, etc. will also affect the outcome.

While developing these approaches and principles, external environmental conditions are also evaluated. The polarizing effects of the current political environment, Ankara's limited experience with citizen councils, the lack of institutionalization of citizen councils, the municipality's weak participation reflex, the decrease in resources due to the Covid-19 Pandemic and the impact of hierarchical and bureaucratic understanding in civil society can be evaluated together and these principles can be adapted when necessary. The greatest strength of Ankara Citizen Council lies in the effective relationship it has established with working groups and assemblies with this understanding.

In the early days of the citizen council, between 2019-2022, when working groups and assemblies had not yet been formed, some of the issues on the city's agenda were proposed to the Greater Ankara Municipality by the executive board in the form of recommendations. A significant number of these recommendations were approved by the municipal council and entered into force. These decisions included the preparation of bicycle and climate action plans in the city, organizing activities for the 100th anniversary of the founding of the Republic of Türkiye, increasing planting and afforestation activities in the city, preparing an agricultural inventory, expanding zero waste activities, establishing art workshops for the disabled, improving parking management in the city, supporting amateur sports and international cultural and artistic activities, establishing a gastronomy center, taking measures for livability-oriented urban planning, and organizing a public health summit.

Unfortunately, when new recommendations were to be proposed to the Greater Ankara Municipality, the Covid-19 Pandemic broke out and the city's priorities radically changed along with the rest of the world. For this reason, the recommendations were waited for a decision by the municipal council and then brought to the agenda through a different method. The experience gained from previous recommendations is that even though there is a council, no results can be obtained without contacting and cooperating with the relevant responsible municipal units. Therefore, starting with the period of the Covid-19 Pandemic, some advisory decisions were directly introduced to the bureaucracy of the municipality rather than being sent to the municipal council and this practice has gradually become established. Apart from this, the proposals of working groups and assemblies will continue to be evaluated in the ordinary citizen council general assemblies.

After these recommendations reached a certain stage and the Covid-19 Pandemic process ended, working groups and assemblies started to work on the recommendations again. It is also important to note an interesting event that took place during these efforts. Although it was not authorized to do so according to the legislation, the audit commission of the Greater Ankara Municipality Assembly, the majority of which was composed of members of the opposition within the municipality, criticized the municipality in its 2022 report, stating in writing that "Ankara Citizen council did not submit a sufficient amount of recommendations". This criticism is on a voluntary organization and its constituents, and it was concluded that this criticism was brought as a result of political conflict between the mayor and the opposition wing in the municipal council. As a result, it was decided that it would be the right action to communicate all the work done to the municipal council without wasting time. At the beginning of 2023, a general assembly was held digitally, and all recommendations were evaluated. The 110 recommendations on different subjects approved after the General Assembly were also forwarded to the Greater Ankara Municipality Assembly. These recommendations were unanimously approved by the

Greater Ankara Municipal Council in October 2023 meeting. A general list of these decisions can be seen in Appendix 1.

Participatory budgeting

Participatory budgeting activities of Ankara Citizen Council started in April 2020 with the formation of a Participatory Democracy Working Group. After the first meetings of the working group, it was approved by the Executive Committee, and the group was attended by academics and experts in the field of participation in civil society. These participants included representatives of innovative internet applications such as Needs Map, academics from universities such as Middle East Technical University (METU) and Hacettepe, and representatives of civil society organizations such as The Development Foundation of Türkiye. The working group spent some time researching the historical roots of participation in the capital city of Ankara and listened to examples of good practices such as the Çiğdemim Association - a community organization which was formed by the residents of Çiğdem neighborhood. Then, current examples of participatory budgeting in the world, such as Paris, were evaluated. Following these studies, a meeting was held with the Deputy Secretary General of Greater Ankara Municipality, and it was decided to work together on participatory budgeting.

As a result of the discussions, it was decided that it would be appropriate to carry out participatory budgeting in two phases. In the first stage, within the scope of the 2021 budget preparation process of Greater Ankara Municipality, official letters were sent to 700 public institutions, universities, associations, foundations, associations, foundations, tradesmen's organizations, and professional associations with the status of public institutions, which mainly include the components of Ankara Citizen council, asking for their opinions on the budget. Opinions were collected with an online form. Upon the public announcement of this consultation process, other institutions and organizations wishing to be involved in the process were also allowed to access the website. Among 300 suggestions, about 40, which were deemed feasible, were forwarded to the relevant departments of the municipality for consideration. During this process, municipality officials and citizen council components came together several times in online meetings.

In the second phase of participatory budgeting, a pilot study was designed as a prelude to budgeting at the neighborhood level. Çiğdemim Association, a component of Ankara Citizen Council, was selected as a representative from a high-income neighborhood in Ankara, and Çiğdemim was paired with the Bahçelievler Neighborhood Mukhtar's Office in Gölbaşı District, a less affluent neighborhood in Ankara. Through a series of meetings, the content and purpose of this pairing were explained to the representatives of both neighborhoods. It was explained that it was very important to transfer what was learned to a disadvantaged neighborhood, as there is a high level of awareness of this kind in Türkiye and Ankara, mostly in high-income neighborhoods. From the very beginning of the process, the Municipality, Ankara Citizen Council, Çiğdemim Association, and Bahçelievler Neighborhood Headman's Office engaged in a process of interaction and learning. Çiğdemim Association and the neighborhood headman's office used participatory methods to identify solutions to problems or requests in their neighborhoods and report these to the municipality.

To set an example, under the leadership of the President of Çiğdemim Association, a survey was prepared and shared with the residents of the neighborhood using the association's extensive social media network and e-mail group. The survey received 340 responses. According to the responses, stray dogs, eco-neighborhood practices to be created by considering the effects of climate change and global warming, and the creation of a public space that elderly and young neighborhood residents can use were prioritized together with the demands for transforming the adjacent housing development area into a neighborhood park.

Çiğdemim Association then shared this method to Gölbaşı Bahçelievler Neighborhood and the demands of the neighborhood residents were collected with a similar method. The Neighborhood Headman's Office and the Gölbaşı Bahçelievler Neighborhood Assistance, Solidarity and Environmental Protection Association reached 261 people through face-to-face interviews with the residents of the neighborhood who came to the Headman's Office. During the interviews, it was determined that the residents who had previously used the place as a home for the elderly in the neighborhood required a new place after the place was given to the association for the relatives of martyrs and veterans, that the women in the neighborhood needed a place to exhibit the food and handicrafts they made at home to contribute to their household income, and that the young people living in the neighborhood needed a library with computer and a place to study.

The representatives of both neighborhoods considered together that a "neighborhood life center" could be requested from the municipality based on the common demands in the neighborhoods. In this regard, some of the design studies that the municipality is also conducting were discussed with the neighborhoods and then it was decided to focus on other needs. To prepare a detailed projection for the stated demands, it was considered to conduct a spending simulation in both neighborhoods. Accordingly, the Municipality asked both neighborhoods to prepare a budget estimate with a market price not exceeding 300,000 TRY. (approx. 10,000 US dollars). Neighborhood representatives narrowed their demands by considering this amount and prepared certain suggestions. In Çiğdem Neighborhood, the most prominent issues were the problem of stray dogs, the utilization of environmental waste, and the improvement of the living conditions of young neighborhood residents. To control stray dogs, it was suggested to focus on sterilization efforts, establish regular feeding points, and start using a mobile application to monitor feeding activities. As an eco-neighborhood practice, in order to make the composting activities carried out in Çiğdemim Neighborhood Garden more efficient and faster, it was envisaged to purchase a composting machine so that more compost could be produced from household and garden waste in a shorter time and to purchase an electric bicycle for the transportation of waste. To address the needs of residents, modern seating units are planned to be placed in various parts of the neighborhood for shopping and relaxing after a walk. As part of the "Governance in the Neighborhood" project, a large LED screen has been proposed to be placed next to Mukhtar's office to ensure better communication with the neighborhood to announce the activities carried out and communicate all activities and events to the neighborhood more effectively.

The representatives of Gölbaşı Bahçelievler Neighborhood also made demands for the problem of stray dogs and the needs of the elderly and young people in the neighborhood. They envisaged the establishment of regular feeding points for stray dogs and monitoring them with a mobile application, the creation of a neighborhood orchard where natural agriculture practices can be carried out and compost produced for this purpose, the provision of seating groups for the use of young neighborhood residents, and the prefabricated construction of a neighborhood library next to the mukhtar's office where children and young people can study, access the internet and read books. Discussions and meetings with ABB officials continued until the end of 2021 for the implementation of these projects. Municipality units benefited to a certain extent from these efforts.

However, the biggest challenge encountered during these activities was the lack of knowledge and responsibility, especially among lower-level municipal employees, about the citizen council and participatory budgeting. To overcome this situation, participatory budgeting activities for municipal employees and citizen council components were reintroduced in the fall of 2021 and activities are still being carried out by the municipality. However, overall, the municipality has not made significant progress on participatory budgeting. Ankara Citizen Council plans to bring the issue of participatory budgeting back to the agenda in time.

Media-based awareness-building

With the rapid development of technological tools, the use and dissemination of electronic participation have become increasingly independent of scale, authority, administrative boundaries, and political power. However, e-participation seems to be an important area of discussion for citizen councils in several ways. First, e-participation eliminates the distinction between representative democracy and direct democracy that emerges in the case of citizen councils and similar participation channels. Examples from around the world and in Türkiye show that virtual assemblies, voting mechanisms, and content-generation platforms can be established without being affected by the limits of legitimacy and legality. This raises the question of how citizen councils and local governments can benefit from these mechanisms. These mechanisms enable citizens to express themselves, but they also come with their language of communication and system of values. On the other hand, the continuity and resilience of such systems may require institutional technical support. The "digital divide" between generations that may apply to citizen councils, where older citizens have more time to participate, may both increase the cost and reduce the effectiveness of e-participation tools.

For this reason, it was decided to utilize social media tools as much as possible, as well as traditional media, in the communication processes of Ankara Citizen Council with both internal stakeholders and the public. This is because current conditions make it difficult to access the necessary capacity to develop effective digital participation tools. First, WhatsApp groups were utilized for the interaction and work of working groups and assemblies. Groups were allowed to create their dynamics, but each group was assigned a secretary from the citizen council office to ensure liaison with the citizen council administration. Each group used this tool with varying degrees of effectiveness. Sometimes, this platform interrupted the work with conflicting and tense communication processes, while most of the time it was a time saver, especially in the coordination of work. At this point, principles of communication and ethical principles have been established for WhatsApp groups.

All the work and activities of the citizen council, which is organized through internal communication, were shared with the public through social media channels, e-mail, local supplements of national newspapers, the YouTube channel of Greater Ankara Municipality, and national television channels. Short videos, posters, and visual designs were prepared, mostly with voluntary contributions and sometimes with the contributions of the secretariat within the council, to ensure more effective dissemination of announcements and news. In all communication activities, careful and sensitive language was used to promote the civic, autonomous, participatory, and inclusive language of the citizen council as a culture. However, these activities often encountered problems caused by the visibility demands of the citizen council's stakeholders and misunderstandings in this regard. Practices such as making the main contributor visible in the activities and obtaining approval from the responsible people for news texts and visuals were carried out. Sharing the Council's activities has increased interest in the activities and expanded the impact of the citizen council. For this reason, the use of effective communication tools within the citizen council has started to be planned as a tool integrated with participation strategies.

Detailed and well-prepared informative reports, activity reports, specially prepared declarations, and statements were also used to share the activities and participation approach of Ankara Citizen Council with the public. Notifications prepared to inform the public on various issues during and after the Covid-19 Pandemic can be given as an example. The 2021 Annual Report is considered to be the largest annual report published by a citizen council to date. In addition, preparations are underway for an innovative "logbook" in which all citizen council activities will be presented, and it is planned to be shared with the public in early 2024. This effective information sharing has also attracted the attention of the academic community; 5 graduate theses and more than 10 academic papers have been published by Ankara Citizen Council. In addition, workshops on various issues concerning the city were organized to raise public awareness.

Active social media and internet addresses of Ankara Citizen Council are given below:

- Ankarakentkonseyi.org.tr
- facebook.com/Ankarakentkonseyi
- twitter. com/ank_kentkonseyi
- youtube.com: Ankara Kent Konseyi
- linkedin.com/company/Ankarakentkonseyi

Lobbying

Considering that there are currently around 1400 municipalities in Türkiye, the fact that the number of citizen councils is about 300 shows that there is a serious problem of knowledge and awareness regarding citizen councils. Until recently, it was thought that the absence of an effective citizen council in the capital city of Ankara, the center of the state, was the reason for this situation. The lack of visibility of citizen councils in Ankara and the fact that they were not recognized by various state institutions caused successful examples of citizen councils across Türkiye to be ignored.

Realizing the need for publicity, the executives of the Union of Citizen Councils of Türkiye and the Citizen Councils Platform of Türkiye, the unofficial supreme unions of citizen councils, have tried to explain the importance of citizen councils for democratic participation by carrying out lobbying activities on this issue at various times. The members of the Union and the Platform visited political parties in power and opposition, various ministries, and local government units and tried to explain the importance and the current problems of citizen councils. In particular, contacts were made with the General Directorate of Local Authorities of the Ministry of Interior, to which citizen councils were previously affiliated, and with the General Directorate of Local Authorities of the Ministry of Environment, Urbanization and Climate Change. Unfortunately, it cannot be said that these efforts have been effective. Due to both the rapid change of staff in the bureaucracy and the fact that the agenda of the current politics is too intense and variable for the citizen councils to notice, these activities have not gone beyond goodwill visits. For this reason, after the establishment of Ankara Citizen Council, members of both the Union and the Platform stated that effective lobbying by the Council could play an important role in the recognition of citizen councils. Aside from lobbying activities, it was believed that running a highly visible and successful citizen council process in Ankara could fulfill this function.

For this reason, Ankara Citizen Council started a process of visiting prominent public authorities in the capital Ankara to convey the meaning and work of citizen councils. In this context, the first visit was made to the President of the Union of Municipalities of Türkiye and Greater Gaziantep Municipality. During the visit, the importance of municipalities establishing citizen councils was explained and the meaning of citizen councils for local democracy and participation was expressed. It was also discussed how to raise awareness on this issue through joint work with the Union of Municipalities of Türkiye. As a visible outcome of this visit, the Union of Municipalities actively supported the 3rd Citizen Councils Symposium organized by the Union of Citizen Councils of Türkiye in Balıkesir in October 2021.

On the other hand, the Chief Ombudsman was visited to evaluate the sanctions on the establishment of citizen councils. During the meeting, the proximity of the basic mission of citizen councils with the Ombudsman's Office was expressed and support was requested for applications to be made to the Ombudsman's Office regarding municipalities that do not establish citizen councils. Following the visit, the Chief Ombudsman attended an event organized by Ankara Citizen Council and addressed representatives of Citizen councils from all over Türkiye, explicitly calling for applications to the Ombudsman's Office regarding mayors who do not establish Citizen councils. Currently, The Union of Citizen Councils of Türkiye is working on a process supported by the Ombudsman's Office. Ankara Citizen Council aims to continue its lobbying activities to make citizen councils better known in Türkiye.

References

Bolton, N & Leach, S. (2002). Strategic planning in local government: A Study of organizational impact and effectiveness, Local Government Studies, 28(4), 1–21.

Clarke, S.E. (2017). Local place-based collaborative governance: Comparing state-centric and society-centric models, Urban Affairs Review, 53(3), 578–602.

Hendriks, F. (2014). Understanding good urban governance: Essentials, shifts and values, Urban Affairs Review, 50(4), 553–576.

5. Strengthening Urban Culture and Identity

Aesthetic negotiation and urban space

One of the most important dimensions of urban life in contemporary cities is the aesthetic dimension. Throughout history, urban space has been the site of artists' aesthetic pursuits and innovative designs. Modern artworks are now connected not only through art galleries and exhibition halls but also through all objects that concern the city and provide an interaction between the user and the city. At this point, the creation of appropriate negotiation processes and a participatory design process for the relationship of design and art with the user has become one of the most prominent discussions. In addition to production-oriented design fields such as architecture, urban planning, landscape architecture, and industrial design, different types of plastic, visual, auditory, and performing arts seek ways to reach and interact with the user and reflect this to the urban space. Sometimes this search, negotiation, and participation process itself can be called a work of art or a performance.

Although the totality of these efforts may not always be fully understood by broader society, new possibilities arise through citizen councils with new approaches they reveal. Considering that one of the biggest problems of cities in urban culture and urban identity is that design products are mass-produced with a mediocre aesthetic understanding that is detached from urbanites in a way that standardizes many cities, the importance of citizen councils taking part in participatory design activities becomes clear. Apart from the opportunities provided by developing technology, participatory design processes and initiatives such as competitions in which citizens can directly participate are critical. The vital role of citizen councils here lies in the fact that they hold the key to making the city a more exciting and intriguing place by bringing citizens together from different disciplines of design and art production and aesthetic pursuits that transcend the mediocre.

Ankara Citizen Council has long been aware that images and symbols in the city have become a means of polarization and therefore has sought to develop a participatory method to reconsider the elements that reflect the language of everyday design. In Ankara, where there are objections, debates, and even conflicts from street signs to urban furniture, from billboards to some important emblems and logos, it is therefore important for the Citizen Council to bring together those who address these issues. These efforts are not isolated from other activities of the Council. Aesthetic values and design processes have encountered and interacted with each other within the Citizen Council. As a result, although not always in a planned manner innovative practices based on participation and negotiation on aesthetics have emerged. Competitions, artistic events, and participatory studies on aesthetic negotiation started to be a part of the design process. Especially with the launch of the Working Groups of Architecture Culture and Planning, Culture and Art, this understanding has developed. Accordingly, Ankara Citizen Council should carry out "aesthetic deliberation" as well as policy deliberation in the process of participation. The main purpose of this deliberation is to reproduce through a qualified aesthetic discussion on design elements in the city that seem doomed to mediocrity, which are mostly created with commercial products and disconnected from their context.

With this understanding, stakeholders within Ankara Citizen Council have tried to contribute to the creation of participatory spaces, starting with the building in which the Citizen Council is located and its immediate surroundings. For this purpose, an idle warehouse in the Citizen Council building was transformed into an exhibition hall for all Ankara citizens, a waste area in Gençlik Parkı (Youth Park) where the Council building is located was designed and implemented as a public open space, and opinions and ideas were generated on many areas in the city. These ideas formed an important basis for design competitions and the resumption of artistic activities in the city. The main elements that constitute this ground can be summarized as follows:

• To show the will to transcend the mediocre in the understanding of urban aesthetics and art,
• Opening a living space for the outlier,
• To create and protect the memory of the culture and arts of the city,
• Supporting the development of sectors related to culture and arts,
• Removal of geographical and urban barriers to access culture and arts.

The implementation of these principles was not only seen as a tool for the dissemination of culture, art, and design in the city but also as an instrument for the strengthening of urban identity and culture with an artistic understanding. Elements of urban culture and identity of the capital city were included in all activities.

Architectural competitions

Competitions are important options for obtaining plans, projects, and designs of urban public spaces that concern the whole city. Administrations have the chance to define the design problems related to the area for which the project is to be obtained, to bring together a pool of experience and knowledge at different scales to obtain solutions to these problems, and to see creative and original solutions alternatives with a high level of creativity through competitions. Thanks to the richness of ideas, they are included in public procurement methods. In addition, through competitions, administrations take on the role of the facilitator in the development of the design and built environment culture of the city and the country by making architecture, design, and planning problems related to local contexts available to a wider audience.

Although interest in competitions and the projects obtained through competitions has been increasing in Türkiye in recent years, it is seen that the number and diversity of competitions are still far behind the desired and equivalent countries, considering the increasing population and urbanization rate. For this reason, many professionals and academics are making special efforts to popularize competitions in our country.

In the capital city of Ankara, Greater Ankara Municipality, which has the authority over the entire city, has not awarded any projects through a competition for a long time. The last competition at the metropolitan scale was held in 2003. This is related to the general approach of the Greater Ankara Municipality in the past years: Unfortunately, the suggestions of universities, academics, and professional chambers to obtain projects through competitions were not taken into consideration by the the mayor at the time. As a result, in many projects and implementations carried out by local governments in the capital, there is no diversity of ideas where the potential of the fields of planning, architecture, urban design, landscape architecture, fine arts, and plastic arts to develop proposals for the city has not been utilized.

To be able to discuss architecture, design, and planning approaches required by the period and to create design awareness, it is imperative to realize a process of communication, dialogue, and sharing between those who govern the city and the architecture, design and planning communities practicing their profession in that city. After the 2019 local elections, with the change of administration in Greater Ankara Municipality, important steps have started to be taken in this sense. Ankara Citizen Council was established on June 29, 2019. Since its establishment, the Council has adopted the principle that the administration should follow a participatory approach to urban problems; the "Culture of Architecture and Planning" Working Group was established in December 2019 with the voluntary support of more than forty academics from various universities in Ankara to realize the implementation of this principle in planning, urban and architectural projects.

The efforts of the Citizen Council, the suggestions of academics from the Architectural Culture and Planning Working Group, professional chambers, and professional organizations were effective in bringing competitions back to the agenda as a participatory method after such a long period; The idea of establishing an Academic Advisory Board under the facilitation of the Department of Cultural and Natural Heritage, with the support of Citizen council, was proposed to the administration to organize competitions for Ankara conservation planning, architecture, urban design, landscape architecture and fine arts when necessary, and to determine the principles and guidelines to be followed in the implementation of practices in certain areas. As a result, the proposal was accepted, and a semi-formal advisory board was formed upon the invitation of the mayor of Greater Ankara Municipality.

The Academic Advisory Board has held a series of voluntary online meetings every week since the fall of 2020, discussing the priority problem areas on the Municipality's agenda and determining the understanding and principles that will be the basis for the competitions and continues to do so. While emphasizing the importance of cooperation with professional chambers, professional organizations, academics, and parties involved in the implementation, the Municipality also tries to develop a common ground on problem areas. This paves the way for participatory and innovative processes, creates new and broad horizons for the future, and opens up Ankara's problems to contributions and ideas on a national scale. The accumulated knowledge of the Academic Advisory Board is utilized to accelerate the competition process and to activate the process of producing the necessary information, documents, and opinions.

Due to the lack of continuity in the administration's competition experience, the Academic Advisory Board also supports the creation of a pool of possible names to be determined by the administration in determining the competition juries, considering many issues such as professional experience, knowledge, gender equality, competition experience, and some practical requirements arising from Covid-19 Pandemic conditions.

Considering the history of competitions in Türkiye, this process is important for its effective use of academic knowledge, and the facilitation of citizen councils and is based entirely on volunteerism. It created an environment for discussion and is considered an unprecedented model. This experience is expected to contribute to planning, urban and architectural problem definition processes, and project production practices based on common sense and dialog both in the capital Ankara and in other cities in Türkiye.

It was agreed that competitions should be seen as an extension of the transparency, accountability, participation, and co-management approach frequently emphasized by the Greater Ankara Municipality administration. From this perspective, the Academic Advisory Board proposed the motto "Ankara through Competition" to define the process to emphasize the trajectory, approach, and importance of a series of competitions for important urban public spaces in the capital. The motto "Ankara through Competitions" emphasizes the concepts of publicness, participation, and common sense concerning the cultural accumulation of the capital city of Ankara, and proposes competitions as a method of obtaining projects, aiming to bring competitions back to the agenda of Ankara.

It is recommended that this process be based on the following principles:

- Respect for the socio-spatial and historical background of the city and legal processes in the definition of competitions
- Cooperation and participation with universities, professional chambers, professional organizations, and professionals in the organization of competitions
- Raising public awareness and awareness of the competitions
- Supporting gender equality in the organization of competitions
- Respecting the professional knowledge, merit, and professional distinctions required by the competitions
- Encouraging the achievement of urban public good through competitions

• Proper documentation of competitions and monitoring possibilities to improve administrative capacity for competitions

In fact, after the 2019 local elections, there has been a significant increase in the number of attempts to design public spaces through competitions in many cities, especially in Istanbul. As seen in the Taksim and Golden Horn Competitions, one of the serious problematics of these competitions was participation. The competition process in Ankara succeeded in creating a lively discussion process by linking the discussion of the competition process with the citizen council from the beginning. As a result, decision-makers, from the mayor to the heads of departments, started to see competition as an approach that could achieve the right outcomes in the design process.

At the beginning of its work, the Academic Advisory Board focused on the Ulus Historic City Center. As the discussions on issues such as the conservation zoning plan and the public spaces around the Ulus Sculpture Square continued, the competition processes began to take shape as the administration conveyed the developments on certain issues and then the academic board conveyed its suggestions. Although this relationship was tense at times, it generally led to productive results due to the openness of the municipality administration. In this sense, the first competition was proposed by the mayor for a monument to be opened for health workers who lost their lives during the Covid-19 Pandemic. Later, a second competition was launched about the use of the burned Modern Çarşı (Modern Bazaar) and the renovation of the Hal (Wholesale Market) Building. Interestingly, while the competitions were ongoing, a process called "Ankara on the Streets" was initiated under the leadership of the seemingly unrelated Zabıta[10] Department, and within this process, a third competition was opened for street signs and the development of a unique Ankara font, since the Head of the Department was also responsible for the municipal firm dealing with the traffic regulation and signs. Because of the upcoming 100th anniversary of the Republic, a competition for a monument in the Dikmen Çaldağı area was envisaged. Finally, a fifth competition was opened for Yüzüncü Yıl Çarşısı (100th Year Bazaar) in Ulus and its immediate surroundings, which the administration had initially planned to demolish and turn into a park. All these competitions are listed on the municipality's website under the name “yarışmaylaAnkara" - Ankara Through Competitions. The members of the academic board have been and continue to be devoted to the design of this page and its logo, and to designing contest posters.

---

[10] A municipal police force charged with seeing that various laws and ordinances are observed, especially those dealing with prices, fair marketing, building construction, and sanitation.

The resumption of the competition process, with the participatory approach of Ankara Citizen Council, has aroused many positive reactions from professional circles in Ankara. Especially in problematic and conflicted areas such as the 100th Year Bazaar, seeking results through competition has led to a deepening of aesthetic deliberation in the city. Ankara Citizen Council's insistence on competitions and efforts to achieve viable outcomes through them will continue.

Public participation and art

Public spaces are of great importance in the formation of culture and identity in cities. The elements of urban culture, the behavioral patterns of citizens, and the images and symbols used in the design of urban public spaces are closely related to the meaning attributed to the public space and how the historical narrative and memory of that space are constructed. Artists and professionals involved in art production discovered public spaces, especially in the twentieth century, and began to realize the potential of meeting with urbanites outside of art galleries and exhibition halls. This led to a transformation in the process of art production. The interaction between the products and installations by known or anonymous artists in public spaces and the relationship they establish with urbanites also serves to make cities livelier and more exciting. For this reason, it has been emphasized that artworks in public spaces, called public art, should be realized through interaction with and participation of urbanites.

This can be seen in examples such as murals on unused walls in the city, installations that enable interaction 24 hours a day, and graffiti, which are increasingly being recognized as works of art. This new field of production, where artistic creativity meets citizen participation, helps urban space to be recognized by city administrations and citizens, and new meanings to be attributed to urban space. On the other hand, the sometimes boring and static cyclical processes of participation are transformed by artistic creativity. Participation in artistic production increases the presence of children, youth, and all segments of society in the participation experience. There are many lessons to be learned from these situations for citizen councils and this unexplored area has the potential to transform the city into a new medium for both art and participation.

With this understanding, Ankara Citizen Council has tried to create a platform where artists and art entrepreneurs in the city come together. Culture and Arts Working Group was established, and independent art initiatives were supported jointly with the municipality. In this context, seasonal opening concerts and theater festivals were organized, participation in modern art fairs was ensured, and artistic products such as murals were encouraged in public spaces in the city. In addition, solidarity programs were developed to support artists in times of crisis such as Covid-19 Pandemic. This environment of artistic solidarity within Ankara Citizen Council has resulted in making the Citizen Council a partner in all activities to be carried out in the city. From film festivals to exhibitions, and concerts to artistic activities in the historic city center, Ankara Citizen Council and its stakeholders have contributed to many activities.

Commemorations and urban memory

October 10th Ankara Garı (Train Station) Competition

On the morning of October 10, 2015, at 10:04 a.m., Türkiye experienced one of the most brutal acts of terrorism. People from all over Türkiye gathered in front of Ankara Train Station for the "Labor, Peace, and Democracy Rally" organized by unions and many other non-governmental organizations. Two suicide bomb attacks were carried out at short intervals at the Station's intersection against the gathering of groups moving to the march area. National mourning was declared after this shocking incident. 103 citizens, including children, lost their lives, more than 450 were injured, and 30 citizens became disabled for life. This event, which has since been known as the October 10th massacre, opened deep wounds in the souls of society and democracy as a crime against humanity and the right to life.

Since its inception, Ankara Citizen Council has been sensitive to the October 10th massacre, one of the most serious social wounds and traumas in the recent history of the capital and has endeavored to support activities that try to raise awareness in this process, especially by supporting the associations established by the families of those who lost their relatives or were harmed in the incident. One of the most important developments in this regard was the opening of the "International Idea and Design Project Competition for Labor, Peace, and Democracy Memorial Square and Place of Remembrance" to organize the place where the massacre took place as a memorial square by a consortium of unions and 10 Ekim-Der (October 10th Association). 39 competitors participated in the competition and in March 2020 the competition was completed. The architect Pınar Kesim Akbaş's team won the first prize with the idea of a landscape arrangement in which 103 trees were planted to represent the people who lost their lives, and a museum was created.

Emek, Barış ve Demokrasi Anıt Meydanı ve Anma Yeri Uluslararası Fikir ve Tasarım Projesi Yarışması	International Ideas and Design Project Competition for Labor, Peace and Democracy Memorial Square and Place
Proje Teslimi Tarihi 24 Şubat 2020	Date of Submission 24 February 2020

www.10ekimanitmeydan.org

Following the completion of the competition, representatives of professional chambers and trade unions presented the projects prepared for the monument to the Greater Ankara Municipality Mayor at the end of October 2020. During the meeting, the delegation requested the support of Greater Ankara Municipality for the implementation, and it was decided that Ankara Citizen Council and Greater Ankara Municipality officials would determine the current technical and administrative situation regarding the implementation and follow up on the implementation process. Afterward, Ankara Citizen Council's President and members of the executive board, the Department of Zoning, the Department of Environmental Protection and Control, and the Department of Transportation of Greater Ankara Municipality gathered under the leadership of the Secretary General of the Municipality and invited the winning team to determine the process. It was determined that the road arrangement to be made at the Station Junction and the landscaping works to be carried out in the Arena Basketball Hall and Turkish State Railway Station parking lot, which were envisaged in the competition, required the affirmations of the relevant institutions. In addition, due to the change in the zoning plan for the Millet Bahçesi (National Garden Project), which includes the Atatürk Cultural Center, 19 Mayıs Sports Complex, and Youth Park, it was stated that permission from the Ministry of Environment, Urbanization, and Climate Change was also required for the construction of the project. Considering these issues regarding the current situation, a consensus was reached on the need to obtain opinions from the relevant institutions before proceeding with the preparation of the application projects. Afterward, the site was examined by the officials of the TMMOB (Union of Chambers of Turkish Engineers and Architects) Chamber of Landscape Architects, and the possible implementation details were evaluated from a technical point of view.

During this process, no comments were received from the institutions regarding the competition. As an indication of the sensitivity towards the site and the competition process regarding the incident, on the proposal of Ankara Citizen Council and under the supervision of the Board of Directors of TMMOB, "Ginkgo Biloba" trees, also known as shrine trees, were placed in pots by Greater Ankara Municipality on October 10, 2021, at the Terminal Junction, which is the commemoration area, as proposed winning project. Unfortunately, these trees were removed by Ankara Governorate on the same day. In this process, Ankara Citizen council components have made a selfless effort for the competition for peace and democracy and its implementation and have followed the process. The issue has been treated with respect and support, not only as an important event in the social history of Türkiye but also as a design process carried out with a common will. The winning Project still waits for the government agencies responsible for the area to permit implementation. Since the event and the competition are seen as part of a deeper political divide, these Agencies seem reluctant to give permission.

100th Anniversary of Turkish Republic Celebrations

The founding of the Republic and historical events have a special significance for the capital, Ankara. The process that started with the arrival of Mustafa Kemal Atatürk, the founder of the Republic of Türkiye, in Ankara on December 27, 1919, brought all the important stages of the establishment process to be experienced. Ankara was declared the capital of the Republic of Türkiye on October 13, 1923, and subsequently, on October 29, 1923, the Republic of Türkiye was established in Ankara. Starting on December 27, 2019, the centenaries of these historical stages were realized. It is important that all stakeholders in the capital act with a supra-political understanding and common sense at these important turning points to ensure that these historical events are properly remembered, realized, and crowned with the active participation of the public. For this reason, efforts have been made to carry out the relevant decision-making processes under the roof of Ankara Citizen Council to act on a common basis. All activities to be carried out by public and non-governmental organizations at these important milestones were designed to leave meaningful traces in public and urban memory.

On December 27, 1919, the day Mustafa Kemal Atatürk arrived in Ankara was called 'Red Day' and the motto 'İyi ki Geldin' (Thank God You Came) was used to celebrate the 100th anniversary of the day when thousands of soldiers rushed to Dikmen ridges to welcome their ancestors. On that day thousands of seğmen in Kızılay, the city center of Ankara, under the leadership of the Council, marched to the parliament in Ulus as they did 100 years ago. In the same context, on the 100th anniversary of the adoption of the National Anthem, the poet Mehmet Akif Ersoy, who wrote its words, was commemorated. 150 cyclists from the Bicycle Assembly took the flag flying on the Anıtkabir flag and brought it to the place where Mehmet Akif Ersoy's grave is located. 2021 was the 100th anniversary of the Battle of Sakarya, the turning point of the national liberation war. For this reason, a Resurrection March was held with thousands of people in Sakarya Village in Polatlı District of Ankara on September 4. Many commemorative events were organized on these important days of our national struggle, reinforcing their place in the memory of the city. For the foundation of the Republic, the 100th-anniversary commemoration was held with different events in 2022 and 2023, and Ankara Citizen council played an important role in the opening of the architectural competition for a commemoration space that will symbolize these important days.

6. Community Engagement

Youth Assembly

Ankara Citizen Council carries out a process similar to that of civil society organizations in the formation of assemblies and working groups specified in the legislation. Working groups, which are required to be established within the Citizen Council, must go through a process where participation is at the highest level. In this context, the formation of a Youth council, demanded by the young citizens of Ankara, took place within this process. In the first stage, those who came together around the youth working group started the process as a platform open to Ankara citizens between the ages of 15 and 30 by conducting regular activities. Youth Working Group not only focused on activities but also produced policies, closely monitored the policies produced by both local and central governments and ensured that young people were involved in policy-making processes.

After a while, the group started to carry out more comprehensive activities on the way to becoming an assembly after reaching 500 stakeholders. Young people came together to discuss how the current youth assembly structure works in Türkiye and around the world. In some of the examples there was individual participation by young people in the specified age range, while in others, structures formed with young representatives of institutions and organizations came to the fore. It was observed that youth assemblies consisting of young representatives of only one institution or organization have deficiencies in terms of participation. In this context, it is necessary to build a mechanism in which every young person living in the city can be involved in the process of Citizen Council Youth Assemblies.

A labor-based volunteer participation approach was implemented, unlike many other youth assemblies. With the construction of a mechanism in the youth working group, those who contribute with their labor the most can be the most involved in the process to ensure the realization of projects. Forums and a youth workshop were organized to analyze the current situation of young people in Ankara. As a result of the meetings with Ankara Citizen Council administration, it was decided to hold the general assembly of Youth Assembly on January 30, 2022.

During the 18 months that have passed since the process started as a youth working group, the youth have embraced the philosophy of the citizen council. The execution of the entire process of the general assembly by young people enabled participation to be realized at a high level. 20 days before the general assembly, it was announced both in the press of Greater Ankara Municipality, in the announcement portals of the Citizen Council, and the social media and network groups of the youth working group, and all young citizens were invited. To determine the functioning and method of the general assembly process, young people came together again and conducted idea workshops. For the process to function properly, non-governmental organizations working on youth in Ankara were contacted, and the involvement of all segments in the process was ensured. All 25 districts of Ankara were contacted, and representatives, one female and one male were invited from the youth organizations of the district citizen councils, if any or from youth organizations in existing municipalities were invited. To ensure both institutional representatives and individual participation in youth assemblies, representatives from civil society and other institutions working in the field of youth were invited to be included in the advisory board.

In addition, invitations were sent to the youth organizations of all political parties to include the political will necessary for the realization of youth policies in the process, and a process was initiated in which young people played a role for young people regardless of ideology, belief, or other differences. While some political parties were eager to be involved in the process, others did not care much about it. In the end, the most democratic participation process possible under the current conditions was built.

On January 30, 2022, the general assembly of the youth council took place at Ankara Chamber of Commerce with a crowd of more than 1,000 enthusiastic people, 600 delegates, and many guests. The Greater Ankara Municipality Mayor Mansur Yavaş, as well as the heads of departments of the Municipality, attended the general assembly. Ankara Citizen Council President, Vice President, and members of the executive board, as well as the councils and working groups within the citizen council, also participated. In the General Assembly, the president of the youth council and 34 executive board members were elected, and the establishment of the youth council was completed. After the official establishment of the Youth Assembly, organizational activities were initiated rapidly. While the membership of young people in the Assembly accelerated with many projects and programs carried out, young people started to seek solutions to their problems in many areas, from the problems of university students to the housing problems of young people. Currently, the number of members of the youth assembly has exceeded 2000. The youth, who are currently working to develop international and national cooperation with the "youth corridor for participation" model, are also the most active body of Ankara Citizen Council.

The Assembly of Disabled Citizens

Since 2019, the "Assembly of Disabled Citizens" has been the first assembly formed by Ankara Citizen Council with the participation of its all members. The establishment process of the Assembly was, in essence, defined as a learning process for the citizen council. For this purpose, a stakeholder analysis was conducted with those who expressed interest among the members of the citizen council and representatives of registered non-governmental organizations in Ankara and specialized in the field of disabled people. A coordination structure was established to organize the first general congregation of the Assembly of Disabled Citizens, which was held with approximately two hundred participants. At the general assembly, considering the needs of different disability groups, a coordination board was formed to fulfill the processes of the Assembly. Then, in the fall of 2021, the General Assembly was held, and the president and executive board were elected. The Assembly of Disabled Citizens has reached a working maturity that reflects this institutional experience.

The Assembly advocates the rights of people with disabilities to live their lives in a manner befitting human dignity and works on revising and integrating legal practices to increase their effectiveness, considering the new institutional structures in social policy and social services. For this purpose, activities are organized to contribute to raising awareness in society, especially during the Covid-19 Pandemic period. In this direction, the goals set by the Disability Council are stated as follows:

- To identify the sociological and psychological problems and obstacles experienced by disabled people living in Ankara in daily life to ensure their participation in social life,
- To carry out educational, sociocultural, and rights-based studies to produce permanent solutions for these problems and disabilities,
- To organize coordinated works with district municipalities and especially Greater Ankara Municipality, on the above-mentioned issues,
- To pave the way for local governments and non-governmental organizations to act together in their work on disability.

To achieve these goals, panels and events were organized; trainings were held for disabled people to learn about their rights; efforts were made to make public transport stops barrier-free; and sign language training was given to drivers in charge of public transport. To raise awareness about the situation of the hearing impaired during the Covid-19 Pandemic period, transparent masks with transparent mouth parts were produced and distributed together with the municipality. In addition, projects to overcome the problems of disabled people were prepared and presented to the municipality. These projects include the following:

- Establishing workshops for disabled people to receive art education,
- Electronic card application to ensure positive discrimination for disabled people in urban services
- Parks and green areas are to be realized by considering the education and needs of disabled people
- Facilitating the participation of people with disabilities in cultural, scientific, and artistic activities
- Conveying various dimensions of disability to society through social media publications

Although the Assembly of Disabled Citizens created an influence in Ankara, there were also criticisms. First, it has been criticized for not pushing hard for policymaking in favor of people with disabilities. There are also arguments about to what extent people with disabilities are in the decision-making process of the Assembly's work, which was seen as overly bureaucratic. These debates are welcomed as signs of institutional learning and change for the good of citizens with disabilities within Ankara Citizen Council.

Rural Development

In line with the National Rural Development Strategy, the Rural Development Working Group aims to contribute to and participate in the creation of the Rural Development Policies of Greater Ankara Municipality with all its members and components to achieve the objectives of developing the rural economy and increasing employment, improving the rural environment and ensuring the sustainability of natural resources. It also has a goal for improving the social and physical infrastructure of rural settlements, developing the human capital of rural society and reducing poverty, and improving institutional capacity for local development, continues its activities by creating a work plan and program to achieve this goal. While the work on rural development is closely related to sustainable development, one of the founding objectives of Ankara Citizen Council, it is also considered important because a significant part of the borders of Greater Ankara Municipality is rural. The working group, which initially consisted of representatives of the Council's member associations on rural development, gradually established close relations with agricultural cooperatives and the municipality's rural development department.

Rural areas should be addressed with policies targeting economic, social, spatial, and environmentally sustainable development based on the development of many sectors in rural areas, involving multi-actor governance with the cooperation of the public, private sector, civil society, and universities, and that solutions can be provided with both sectoral and spatial approaches in rural areas. In this context, new approaches have emerged that aim to ensure the competitiveness of rural areas, utilize local assets, benefit from unused resources, diversify rural economies (rural tourism, manufacturing industry, ICT industry sectors), and use new investment instruments. Actors are at all levels of governance: supranational, national, regional, and local, as well as local stakeholders (public, private, and non-governmental organizations). Rural Development Working Group, which was established within Ankara Citizen Council started its work by holding its first meeting on January 19, 2020, with the call made by the Executive Board to ensure the contribution of these new approaches to rural development and the needs and demands of rural Ankara to local government policies.

Since the beginning of 2021, the Rural Development Working Group has led the establishment of cooperation between relevant institutions and NGOs for the "2021 Ankara Focused" support program of the United Nations Development Program Small Grants Program (UNDP-GEF-SGP), to ensure maximum participation of civil society in the calling program and more project production throughout Ankara. In this context, in addition to organizing information meetings where all parties came together, it participated in promotions and meetings organized by stakeholders.

Upon the request of the United Nations Development Programme Small Grants Fund (UNDP-GEF-SGP) National Coordinator and at the initiative of Ankara Forum Association, a coordination meeting was held on October 22, 2020, at Ankara Citizen Council. Council members, the Development Foundation of Türkiye, Ankara Forum Association representatives, and the UNDP-GEF-SGP National Coordinator participated in the Meeting. In the said meeting, within the scope of the UNDP-GEF-SGP "2021 Ankara Focused" support program, it was decided that the coordination of the support program with civil society and participating institutions will be carried out by Ankara Citizen Council (Rural Development Working Group) to ensure maximum participation of civil society in the call program and more applications in Ankara.

The council carried out cooperation and coordination activities to ensure the support of the 'Tohumluk Foundation', also a component of the Working Group, and Greater Ankara Municipality for the implementation of a series of educational, cultural, and development-oriented projects planned by Ankara Cultural Association, a component of the Working Group, in Kızılcahamam Taşlıca Village.

The Rural Development Working Group organized meetings for local cooperation to support the projects on "Blue and Green Areas Governance System at Ankara Scale" and "Protection of Salt Lake Ecological System". The Group also took part in the other working groups for the planning and implementation of the project work on "Respect for Water Meetings", which was initiated together with the AKK Environment and Zero Waste Working Group and the AKK Public Health Working Group and contributed to cooperatives and participated in all stages.

At the request of the Greater Ankara Municipality Rural Services Department, Greater Ankara Municipality organized a working meeting on cooperation on "cooperatives' funding activities" and established a ground for cooperation with organizations such as the Development Foundation of Türkiye, Ankara Development Agency, the United Nations Food Organization (FAO), and the United Nations Development Programme Small Grants Program (UNDP-GEF-SGP) for the same purpose.

A working meeting was organized to prepare the ground for civil organizations such as Beştepe College, Utopia Science Center, and Local Development Association, which are working on "Providing Agriculture, Environment, Nature, and Perm Culture Education for Children" and "Virtual Market Application for Women's Cooperatives", to inform the relevant units of Greater

Ankara Municipality about their work, and an environment was provided for all relevant parties to be aware of each other and cooperate. The project on "Ecological Agriculture and Access to Safe Food" was carried out by the Council's component Four Seasons Ecology Association together with the Sustainable Living Association.

In general, the rural development working group ensured that the citizen council extended to rural areas outside the city and established partnerships with stakeholders in rural areas. It brought many issues, such as food security, rural depopulation, and production problems, to the city's agenda.

Gender Equality

Within the structure of citizen councils in Türkiye, gender issues are highly controversial. Gender issues may be seen as taboo, whereas it is imperative to work for the solution of women's problems in public life. Although other aspects of gender are also addressed in opposition municipalities, it can be said that gender equality is generally addressed in the context of "strengthening women's social position and equal rights". It is also observed that "women's assemblies" are included in the legislation on citizen councils. However, it is difficult to say that women's assemblies have been able to raise sufficient awareness within citizen councils. In this regard, it is often criticized that women's assemblies have turned into a focus of political power and that they do not contribute sufficiently to women's struggle for their rights.

Ankara Citizen Council has kept the issue of gender equality on the agenda since its establishment and has endeavored to ensure equal representation, especially in the formation of representative organs such as executive boards. In addition, the approach has been to provide training for all to be aware of the issue. While the Covid-19 Pandemic conditions were ongoing, all executives participated in a three-day, certified training online. Thanks to experienced trainers and a competent program, all participants were able to follow the lessons at the highest level and interactively. Participants stated that the training was eye-opening on many issues and made them aware of the discrimination we are subjected to without even realizing it.

The establishment of a women's assembly within Ankara Citizen Council has not been realized despite being discussed for a long time. There have been discussions on the formation of a women's assembly in a citizen council at the scale of Ankara with a design that can represent all segments, but these have not been concluded. Since it was understood that the requests for initiatives by various political parties and civil society organizations on this issue were mostly directed towards narrow political goals, the Council's executive board's proposals to first build capacity and a method to include all women initiatives at the metropolitan scale this issue were not accepted by those who took these initiatives. On the other hand, the Council did not take part in the different gender debates, which have recently been the subject of great political conflicts in Turkish society and did not engage in any activities on this issue. This was because the citizen council was very young and avoided engaging in corrosive debates on such issues.

Nevertheless, Ankara Citizen Council has organized various activities and training for women to be more active in social life and has supported civil society organizations and initiatives operating in this field. One of the most important of these is the hosting and support provided during the Covid-19 Pandemic for Uçan Süpürge "Flying

Broom Women's Film Festival", which has been supported and realized by the women's movement in Ankara for more than 25 years. This support continued afterward, and the situation of women was also considered in all kinds of activities of the citizen council.

Crisis and Solidarity

In line with the principle of the social state, citizen councils aim at solidarity with all urbanites, especially those who are subjected to social inequality. They offer suggestions and set goals to solve inequalities as an urban problem through social solidarity. In this respect, innovative approaches such as mutual aid, crowdfunding, solidarity networks, and the solidarity and social support mechanisms of municipalities are of interest to citizen councils. Future discussions of the citizen councils include the consideration of solidarity within the framework of solidarity economies, which are ultimately considered within the framework of sustainable development.

In addition, it is seen that citizen councils have a serious potential for organizing solidarity in times of disaster and crisis, both inside and outside the city, by bringing together those in need. Especially when citizen councils, which have the chance to reach a wide range of stakeholders, initiate this organization, people trust to make the necessary sacrifices for others. Here, a new culture of solidarity, facilitated using new technologies and relationships of trust established before the disaster, can be more effective. Since its establishment, Ankara Citizen Council has become a focal point of solidarity in many crises and disasters that took place in Ankara or other areas of Türkiye. During the Covid-19 Pandemic that affected the whole world, forest fires, floods, and earthquakes that affected Türkiye, Ankara Citizen Council has always actively organized its stakeholders and rushed to the aid of those in need.

Covid-19 Pandemic

During the Covid-19 Pandemic, which has been effective since March 2020, Ankara Citizen Council, with all its components, has made efforts to spread solidarity throughout the city. During the Covid-19 Pandemic, the innovative contributions of Ankara Citizen Council components in supporting citizens over the age of 65 and vulnerable segments of society constituted an important stage in understanding the importance of the Citizen Council. The citizen council aims to continue its work towards the goal of making city governance participatory and to work on developing participatory management approaches based on cooperation, coordination, and negotiation in Ankara, which has been lagging in this regard for a very long time. The need for the citizen council to strive for the establishment of a bottom-up participatory process beyond institutional stakeholders, starting at the level of citizens, apartment blocks, housing estates, streets, neighborhoods, and districts, is frequently expressed in the council's work.

Citizen councils in Türkiye have shown different reflexes in the face of Covid-19 Pandemic conditions. It is observed that the activities of the citizen councils, whose level of participation and volunteerism was formed with loose ties and whose relations with the local government developed in the form of a dependency have completely stopped during the Covid-19 Pandemic period. This is not surprising for the experience of citizen councils in Türkiye, where face-to-face human relations and collective interaction are particularly important. However, it is observed that some citizen councils, on the contrary, increased their level of participation and solidarity, and emphasized an understanding based on participation and solidarity to overcome the problems that emerged during the Covid-19 Pandemic. In this case, another defining variable is the central administration. The fact that the role of the central administration in the fight against the Covid-19 Pandemic, especially at the level of local governments, is very large, and even though there are sometimes conflicting processes between local governments and the central administration, has highlighted the efforts of citizen councils to bring common sense to the fore. Here, for example, citizen councils can be accepted as observer members to the Provincial Covid-19 Pandemic Committees established in local government units controlled by the central government, but where opposition municipalities exist, such applications are usually rejected. In conclusion, Ankara Citizen Council, with fresh excitement and a long-standing expectation of great participation, has set important examples of good practices during the Covid-19 Pandemic period considering the conflict between the central administration and local governments. Although each of these examples is worth analyzing on its own, the most prominent topics are the following:

- Immediately after the official measures taken by the state regarding the Covid-19 Pandemic process were announced, Ankara Citizen Council suspended its normal functioning and meetings and started to work on eliminating the effects of the Covid-19 Pandemic period with solidarity and participation. In this sense, all communication channels were used effectively, and the meetings of working groups and assemblies were moved to the virtual environment via Zoom. Active facilitation methods were used to ensure the effectiveness of the meetings.
- Following the restriction on citizens over 65 years of age from going out on the streets, Ankara Moto Courier Federation, a component of the Citizen

Council, and Greater Ankara Municipality brought together local supermarket chains to provide services to homes. In this sense, Ankara Citizen Council acted as a bridge to convey the ideas of its constituents on solidarity to local governments. This innovative practice continued for about 4 months, after which it was observed that local tradesmen and grocery stores in the city built their capacities for these services.

- Through the components in the city, deprived segments were identified and reported to Greater Ankara Municipality for assistance. Here, Ankara Citizen Council was one of the first to identify the situation of groups such as music producers in Türkiye.
- To increase the morale and motivation of the population staying at home in Ankara, videos and posts on urban awareness were published through social media. All these posts were provided by the voluntary efforts of members and components of the citizen council and no financial resources were used.
- Social media posts were shared to ensure that citizens duly complied with the measures taken during the Covid-19 Pandemic. Again, all the posts were provided by the voluntary efforts of the members and components of the citizen council, and no financial resources were used.

- Especially during the period of curfews in 2020, a "Declaration on the rules to be applied in construction during the Covid-19 Pandemic period" was published to invoke the necessary sensitivity to cultural heritage and urban public spaces in construction activities carried out in areas such as Saraçoğlu Neighborhood and Güvenpark in Ankara. Thus, advocacy activities continued during the Covid-19 Pandemic.
- During the Covid-19 Pandemic, the "Most Beautiful Balcony Contest" was organized in cooperation with Greater Ankara Municipality. This contest provided moral support for the beautification of the living environment of citizens staying at home.
- On important days such as the 100th Anniversary of the opening of the Grand National Assembly of Türkiye (TBMM), and national holidays such as Youth and Sports Day on May 19 and Mother's Day, which coincided with the Covid-19 Pandemic period, activities were carried out on social media by exchanging views with the constituents, and activities were supported by other institutions and organizations.
- Nearly 1,000 disinfectants, 90,000 masks, and flower and vegetable seedlings procured from Greater Ankara Municipality were distributed to members to boost their morale during their stay at

home. For members over 65, these materials were delivered to their homes.

- Again, during the Covid-19 Pandemic period, warning notices were prepared and shared with the public together with public health experts to use the correct methods in disinfection activities to be carried out in public places in the city and to prevent environmental pollution.
- In 2021, workshops were organized to identify the effects of the Covid-19 Pandemic on economic sectors and social segments, and the identified problem areas were shared with the public and decision-makers. Workshops with the food and beverage sector, music producers, and young people are among the most important of these activities.
- In addition, the report titled "Ten vital agendas for Covid-19 Pandemic-resilient cities" was shared with the public to follow longer-term and correct urban policies during the Covid-19 Pandemic.
- Apart from all these, events were organized on topics such as water, urban design, and urban transportation, which are indirectly related to the measures taken against the Covid-19 Pandemic.
- Academic studies have tried to enlighten the public on the structural participatory measures to be taken against the Covid-19 Pandemic.

For Ankara Citizen Council, the Covid-19 Pandemic period became a means of coming together and creating channels of solidarity during the period of institutionalization and maturation after its establishment. In this sense, it carried out activities that were followed with interest from many parts of Türkiye. Although organizational aspects of citizen councils remain in the background considering that they do not have direct executive duties in such crisis periods, it should not be forgotten that extraordinary conditions create unique participation demands and experiences.

The experience of Ankara Citizen Council during the Covid-19 Pandemic has set an important example of what kind of contributions citizen councils can make when mobilizing appropriate resources with the right principles. With this approach, it was possible to become an effective element of crisis management without getting involved in the debates of the daily political sphere. The environment of trust and common sense within the citizen council enabled the council components to come together around this solidarity approach to discuss creative and innovative solutions, and even to put forward solutions that could mobilize the local government. However, it is undeniable that there is a problem area arising from the culture of participation in Türkiye. This problem is that participatory activities are reduced to polarized options, perceived as part of individual judgments and as a result, there is no room for deliberation on urban problems. The experience of Ankara Citizen Council provides important lessons for addressing this problem. In this experience, openness, transparency, horizontal organization, allowing constituents to express themselves, and providing an interface between local government and stakeholders in the city play an important role.

Kahramanmaraş Earthquake and Ankara Citizen Council

During and after the Covid-19 Pandemic, a culture of solidarity emerged among the components of Ankara Citizen Council during the flood disasters and forest fires across Türkiye. Different stakeholders organized aid campaigns to deliver aid to disaster areas. These experiences enabled Ankara Citizen Council to carry out a multi-organized and systematic solidarity process during the devastating earthquake in 2023.

On February 6, 2023, in the face of the earthquake that affected 11 provinces in the east of Türkiye and their surroundings and shook the whole of Türkiye deeply, Ankara Citizen Council quickly came together with its components and started to work to meet the needs of the post-earthquake period. Founded in June 2019, Ankara Citizen Council, which is the most widely participated council in Türkiye with its 1800 components and 5000 volunteers, has called on all of Ankara to solidarity with its four years of experience since the news of the earthquake and has created a movement that is gradually growing in momentum. Ankara Citizen Council has organized similar solidarity activities in the past, such as providing supplies and sending them to fire zones after forest fires on the Aegean and Mediterranean coasts, bringing together Türkiye's leading metropolitan mayors and citizen councils on an online platform for solidarity by Ankara Citizen council after the Izmir Earthquake, and carrying out important work on innovative forms of solidarity during the Covid-19 Pandemic. After the 2023 earthquake, a solidarity process was initiated and successfully carried out through the Başkent Youth Assembly, the official body of Ankara Citizen Council, where approximately 1,000 young people were members voluntarily. Important topics and information about this solidarity process are presented in Appendix 2.

While these efforts were ongoing, Ankara Citizen Council assumed the Presidency of the Citizen Councils of Türkiye and started to work on raising earthquake awareness across Türkiye. First, a very special meeting titled "4.17", referring to the time of the earthquake, was organized to share experiences about what happened in the earthquake, bringing together all stakeholders who suffered from the earthquake. Then, with the contributions of academics and different citizen councils, a declaration was published on how citizen councils should act during and after disasters. After these efforts, the work continued to meet the needs of earthquake victims who came to the capital Ankara. In the aftermath of such a devastating disaster, Ankara Citizen Council emphasized the importance of solidarity but also stressed that what is essential is urbanization processes based on scientific knowledge and the creation of resilient cities. Above all, this solidarity process in the aftermath of the earthquake has set an important example for Türkiye on the potential of citizen councils in times of crisis.

7. Quality of Life

Creating public space for citizen participation

Ankara Citizen Council building and Gençlik Parkı (Youth Park) event area

The first issue that every citizen council in Türkiye must face after its establishment is finding and allocating a council building. This may sometimes create tension between citizen councils and municipalities. As is often the case with most municipal buildings, citizen council buildings are far from being as functional as they need to be for work. In very few cases, citizen councils have been allocated to a space that can respond to the diversity of their activities and meet their architectural and aesthetic needs.

Following the establishment of Ankara Citizen Council, the search for a building where the council's activities would be carried out began. While evaluating various alternatives, issues such as accessibility, functionality, and capacity were considered. However, it became clear that many of the venues considered had serious problems. First of all, it was regretfully learned that many buildings known to belong to Greater Ankara Municipality before the elections were transferred to various ministries and district municipalities. Among these was the former Ankara Zoning Directorate building opposite Güven Park, which was used by Ankara Citizen Council in the past. However, the land and the building where the zoning directorate building was located were of historical significance as the first registered building belonging to a zoning directorate in the Republic of Türkiye. Some other alternatives were either not very accessible or required significant investment. As a result, it was decided that Ankara Citizen Council would start to serve in the reception hall of Greater Ankara Municipality, located at the corner of Youth Park - a central and historic park, which was planned with the establishment of Ankara as the capital. Constructed during the renovation of the park in 2009, this historic-looking building was at first unfamiliar with its extravagant and eclectic decorations and its impractical technical infrastructure, but over time it was embraced by the citizen council's constituents. The citizen council's executive also began to look for ways to make the best and most effective use of the building's facilities, trying to manage the growing number of members and the demands of its constituents.

During this process, many problems related to the building and the park were realized. First of all, just before the 2019 local elections, the land of Youth Park was transferred to a company affiliated with the Under secretariat of Treasury, and then the park was transferred to the Ministry of

Environment, Urbanization, and Climate Change. Furthermore, the inclusion of Youth Park within the scope of the ongoing Millet Bahçesi (National Garden) project in Ankara raises questions about the fate of the park. The fact that one of the most important parks in the history of the Republic, which has been maintained and operated by the Greater Ankara Municipality for more than fifty years, has been handled in this way has caused the Citizen council to pay close attention to the park. As a result of the observations made, it has been observed that the user profile of the park has completely changed, especially after the park revision in 2009; it has been observed that not all segments of the capital city of Ankara use the park anymore and that the businesses in the park and certain parts of the park have been associated with illegal and illegitimate activities in the eyes of the public. The occupation by the operators of the rented areas in the park and their going beyond the space allocated to them in the park cause many problems, especially in terms of security and perception. The situation of Youth Park was frequently brought up and solutions were discussed by working groups and the executive committee established in the citizen council.

Especially with the launch of the Architecture Culture and Planning and Culture and Art Working Groups, Ankara Citizen Council decided to adopt "aesthetic deliberation" as well as policy deliberation in the process of participation.

The main purpose of this deliberation is to reproduce through a qualified aesthetic debate the design elements in the city that seem doomed to mediocrity, which are mostly commercial products and disconnected from their context. At some point, these discussions began to be evaluated together with the context of Youth Park, in which Ankara Citizen Council is located, and the importance of the Council's participatory intervention for the future of the park began to be discussed.

The developments in Youth Park during the Covid-19 Pandemic period created the ground for the development of some ideas for some arrangements that could be made in the park. It was observed that a significant number of commercial enterprises in the park went bankrupt due to the Covid-19 Pandemic and vacated the spaces they rented. Especially after a business located right next to the council building vacated the space, the idea of designing an open-air activity area that would carry and strengthen participation began to take shape. It was thought that this event space could contribute to meeting the need for an outdoor gathering space during the Covid-19 Pandemic, create a participatory gathering and interaction space, and enrich the user involvement of Youth Park by creating a new space for the use of the citizen council components. The planning of this design effort was carried out in collaboration with the youth group Ankara AKS, which is a component of Ankara Citizen Council and brings together young people in Ankara who have university degrees in design.

Volunteer young architects and designers from Ankara AKS group worked with Ankara Citizen Council and the Department of Urban Aesthetics of Greater Ankara Municipality to design the site. The principles of sustainable design and re-functionalization of the area following the founding philosophy of Youth Park were adopted. For this purpose, it was aimed to re-functionalize the existing membrane canopies and closed commercial units in the area and to redesign the open space in the area with a stage, exhibition area, wooden seating groups, and a children's playground. The design takes into account the vista of the plane tree in the area, which is as old as the park, to Anıtkabir and the designs of Herman Jansen, the designer of the park. After the design was approved, Ankara AKS students completed the implementation process with the materials found in the warehouses of Greater Ankara Municipality and with the help of workers of the Municipality. This implementation, which was realized with almost no expenditure, has become a symbol of the virtue of solidarity and volunteerism for all components of Ankara Citizen Council. To make this selfless effort memorable, the names of all employees and students who contributed to the process were written on one of the membrane columns in the Event Area. Landscape descriptions were hung on all the trees in the area, and an exhibition of old photographs of the Youth Park was placed in the exhibition area. The closed commercial unit was transformed into a meeting room and office with the designs of the students, and Herman Jansen's drawings of the Youth Park and an honor notebook were placed at the entrance, for visitors to write down their impressions.

Since the opening of the Youth Park activity area, many events and meetings have been organized by Ankara Citizen council components during the Covid-19 Pandemic period. As a result of these activities, it is observed that awareness has been created among the citizen council components and those who use the park. This awareness is expected to increase further in the coming years. The fact that people passing through the park during the events approach the area by sight or hearing and that children and young people use this area at all hours of the day are seen as one of the best indicators that the goal has been achieved.

Considering that exhibitions are one of the main types of activities to be carried out by a citizen council for various purposes, the idea of building an exhibition hall in the council building was formed after a while. For this purpose, it was decided to transform a storage area in the basement of the council building, which also has a level entrance from the back door, into an exhibition hall. It was decided that this area, through which the infrastructure pipes of the building mostly pass, could be transformed making the infrastructure visible, which recently became popular. Interventions such as transferring some of the infrastructure pipes of the warehouse, effectively constructing an exhibition space in the area, and painting the area in black and dark gray tones in terms of exhibition visuality were considered. These interventions were implemented with materials provided by the municipality. In addition, the necessary flooring and relief of Ankara Citizen Council logo were installed so that the area could be used as a meeting hall when necessary.

Ankara Citizen Council event space and the exhibition hall were opened simultaneously in the late summer of 2020.

The first exhibition in the exhibition hall was "Architectural Works of the Republican Era", which was prepared and realized by the Architects Association in 1927, about the fate of the buildings of the capital built during the republican period. It was decided that this exhibition would remain in the exhibition hall permanently. In addition, various exhibitions of the working groups and assemblies and the works of the components have been exhibited in the exhibition hall at various times over time, and the area is also used as a venue for Greater Ankara Municipality’s (ABB) TV programs and as a live broadcasting area for Ankara Citizen council Urban Workshops.

Çubuk Barajı (Çubuk Dam) Recreation Area

One of the most important features of urban life should be that citizens living in the city and people with specific expertise have an awareness and a say in the decisions and practices taken in the city. However, there needs to be a participatory channel for these opinions to reach decision-makers and implementers and be reflected in practice. In many cases, these different views become available for discussion through communication tools. Yet, for these to influence practice, there needs to be an environment in which details can be discussed and, if necessary, made, broken down, or even abandoned.

In this respect, the process of protecting the historic Çubuk Dam and transforming it into a recreation area constitutes an important example for Ankara Citizen council. In the past two decades, the lack of contemporary approaches to the tangible and intangible cultural heritage of the Republican era in Ankara has caused serious damage to the cultural heritage of the city. The destruction of various Republican-era architectural monuments and the misuse of areas such as Atatürk Orman Çiftliği (Atatürk Forest Farm) can be counted among the examples. Among these, the demolition of Baraj Gazinosu (Dam Casino), which was built with national resources and local engineers during the Republican era and played an important role in supplying water to the infrastructure system of the capital, was a painful case. The previous municipal administration had planned to turn the dam area into a prehistoric animal and science park with stuffed animals. For this purpose, various design studies have been carried out since 2009 and it was envisaged to remove the landfill accumulated in the body of the dam. After the 2019 local elections, all these proposals were abandoned and the process of transforming the area into a public recreation area was initiated. Undoubtedly, the need for urban open space that emerged during the Covid-19 Pandemic period was also effective in this.

One of the priorities of Ankara Citizen council since its establishment in June 2019 has been to address the republican heritage of the capital as an element of urban identity. For this reason, the process of transforming Çubuk Dam into a recreational area could perhaps be the first stage of compensating for the losses of the past and starting to value the city's essential identity elements, so experts and executive committee members of the citizen council and the president of the citizen council, also a landscape designer, started to closely monitor the process. The idea of municipal authorities in the first phase was to deal with the area with a landscape arrangement without major structural interventions, to carry out the necessary repairs to the body of the dam and the water channel, and to place commercial and other service elements to meet daily needs. Although Dam Casino was not on the agenda, it was envisaged that the Atatürk House would be organized as an exhibition hall and that the dam would hold water after the necessary infrastructure arrangements.

In 2019 and 2020, members of the Executive Board of Ankara Citizen council and its constituents visited the area with authorities and tried to contribute to the maturation of the practices. The suggestions included the following: 1. Improving the quality of landscape applications, 2. Preserving and exhibiting the historical and cultural heritage elements in the area, 3. Reconstruction of the casino, 4. Improving the use and functionality of the area, 5. Contributing to the organization of the opening process. The meetings held during these visits were occasionally attended by experts in the field, such as the management of the TMMOB Chamber of Landscape Architects and an application close to the original use of the dam was realized to a large extent.

Throughout these visits, a completely voluntary process of participation was carried out between the officials of the implementing company ANFA, the Department of Environmental Protection and Control, the Department of Public Works, and Ankara Citizen Council. This participation has resulted in some additional outcomes, such as the creation of a permanent exhibition in the exhibition hall that tells the history of the dam. Çubuk Dam Recreation Area was inaugurated with a glorious ceremony on October 29, 2020, and then started to be used with great interest by the citizens of Ankara. After the completion of the necessary infrastructure and engineering works, the dam body began to hold water at the end of 2021. Ankara Citizen council is still persistently following the process of rebuilding the demolished casino.

Participation in the renovation of the Ulus Historical City Center

Renewal and revitalization of the historical and commercial centers of cities are imperative for a vivid urban life. Although they are generally considered technical and design-oriented studies, the opinions of the tradesmen and city dwellers living in these areas regarding the arrangements to be made are closely related to the success of the implementation of urban design and renovation works initiated by Greater Ankara Municipality in Ulus Historic City Center, workshops were held to get the opinions of the public and tradesmen. Draft projects on Posta and Anafartalar Streets were shared with tradesmen, some of whom are members of Ankara Citizen council, and opinions were exchanged. In the two workshops, academics, local shopkeepers, and bureaucrats were brought together with the facilitation of Ankara Citizen council, and their opinions on the projects were received. After these meetings, which were very effective in the evaluation and acceptance of the projects by the public, the projects reached the implementation stage in 2023.

Ankara on the Street Project

Ankara Citizen Council has long been aware that images and symbols in the city have become a means of polarization and therefore has sought to develop a participatory method to reconsider the elements that reflect the language of everyday life. In Ankara, where there are objections, debates, and even conflicts from street signs to urban furniture, from billboards to some important emblems and logos, it is therefore important for the Council to bring together those who are the addressees of the issue. These efforts are not isolated from the other activities of the Citizen Council. Aesthetic values and design processes have encountered and interacted with each other within the Citizen Council. As a result, although not always in a planned manner, unexpected practices based on participation and negotiation on aesthetics and carried out through new relationships between actors have emerged. One of the best examples of this is Ankara on the Street program.

The work, which was initially unnamed as such, started with a meeting held within Ankara Citizen Council to determine the standards of outdoor billboards on buildings in the city center. In this meeting, where the Greater

Ankara Municipality's Department of Police, non-governmental organizations such as the Outdoor Advertising Association, Ankara Chamber of Commerce's professional committee, academics from the field of architecture and professional organizations were represented, outdoor directions and advertising displays in the city began to be discussed. In time, with the suggestion of the advertisers participating in this meeting, an approach called "Ankara on the Street" was proposed and accepted in a more holistic framework. With this program, the subject matter of the meetings began to diverge, as the subtleties and symbols of daily life in the city were addressed with a new story and message. The topics discussed were no longer just billboards, but the design of street signs and even the creation of a font specific to the capital city. In the same period, the initiation of competitions within the Citizen Council led to the conclusion that the competition method could be followed in these matters as well. Thus, the first product of these efforts was "Ankara on the Street". This competition, one of the first of its kind, was also published on the website https://yarismayla.Ankara.bel.tr/ (Ankara through Competition).

With this competition, it is aimed to obtain signboards and billboards and an original font. The subject of the competition requires an interdisciplinary approach (i.e., architecture, industrial design, industrial product design, interior architecture, environmental design, graphic design, and landscape architecture). The competition is a free, national, single-stage, and collaborative project competition. It is the work of designing the neighborhood street and street name signs, building door numbers, and architectural identification signs of the buildings in the central and affiliated districts of Ankara province, using a design and font that is unique to Ankara with an understanding that will carry the traces of the first century of our Republic to the second century.

The competition was finalized in August 2021 and a unique font for the capital Ankara was selected. The winner was a typeface designed based on the writing styles of the republican period. The typeface is now available for download in font libraries and is being used on important signs of the Municipality. For street signs, the 3 different designs most liked by the jury were submitted to public voting. The option with white text on a burgundy background received the majority of votes from the public. Currently, municipal teams are replacing all street and avenue signs in Ankara.

After the competition, with the contribution of advertisers and artists associated with the group that carried out these works, work on street art was initiated as part of Ankara on the Street. Murals were painted by artists on the retaining walls of the central bus station (AŞTİ) in a festival atmosphere. With this event, Greater Ankara Municipality

realized a public art event on this scale for the first time in Ankara.

Environmental Awareness and Public Health

Respect for water

One of the most controversial issues regarding citizen councils is politics. According to some, citizen councils are political structures and represent the balance of power at the local level. Others argue that citizen councils cannot be excluded from power relations and that their voluntary nature predisposes them to long-term proper policy debates. The discussions of Ankara Citizen council on the water issue have also been instructive in terms of shaping a political debate on water resources and infrastructure in Ankara.

Starting from the end of 2019, the current administration's request for borrowing authority in Greater Ankara Municipality Assembly, mainly to renew the clean water and sewerage infrastructure, has caused serious debates. Following these discussions, the Executive Board of Ankara Citizen Council decided to establish the " Right to Water Working Group" as a joint and temporary initiative of the Public Health Working Group and Environment and Zero Waste Working Group to address the water policy in Ankara. In this context, public visits were made to the facilities of Ankara Water and Sewerage Administration (ASKİ), and on the other hand, academicians who are experts in their fields came together to evaluate how water policy should be handled. As a result of these studies, it was decided to carry out studies within the framework of the concept of "respect for water". In this way, a fundamental problem area related to daily politics in the city could be the subject of a separate policy accumulation. The Respect for Water Meetings were organized as panels in 2021, 2022 and 2023. Bureaucrats and academics participated in the panels and the importance of the right to water and the water footprint of the city was evaluated in these meetings.

Public health

The Public Health Working Group was established just before the Covid-19 Pandemic. The group, which continued its work online during the Covid-19 Pandemic, gradually increased its dynamism in this period. Because the subject of the group was of vital importance and the working method was based on the principle of participation. In the development process of the Working Group, the main theme of "urban health" provided a conceptual framework in which every citizen and every non-governmental organization could contribute by assuming responsibility for public health issues. This framework also revealed the need to improve the Working Group's communication channels with the public. Thus, the idea was born to organize periodic online events where guests from different fields of expertise, sectors, institutions, and organizations could express their views and communicate with society through interviews. This communication event was named "Gatherings" due to its connotations of participation, togetherness, and coherence. At the same time, the Gatherings functioned to nourish the dynamism of the Working Group, enable it to form opinions in various fields, and support the development of a common approach and common language among members from different fields of experience and profession. From 2020 until the end of 2022, nearly 30 online and face-to-face meetings were organized and views of experts on various aspects of public health were shared with the public.

Cycling

Ankara, the capital of the Republic, was a city without bicycle lanes for transportation purposes except for some recreational areas. This situation, which does not befit a capital city, triggered the process of starting the planning of bicycle paths in Ankara, which should exist in a modern city. Ankara Citizen council has made efforts to promote cycling as a means of transportation in the city through the established bicycle council. To this end, it has contributed to transportation planning studies, participated in the 53 km bicycle path project as a facilitator and guided participatory processes, contributed to the study on Priority Bicycle Network within the scope of Decarbonization of Urban Transportation in Ankara and Non-Motorized Transportation Types Project prepared by the Electricity, Gas and Bus Operations (EGO) General Directorate and advocated for cyclists and bicycle paths. Within the scope of European Mobility Week and on important days, activities were organized with the Greater Ankara Municipality, and bicycle empathy training was given to drivers of public transport.

Climate action planning

The effects of the global climate crisis are being felt more and more in large cities and urbanites. One of the main causes of the climate crisis is the lifestyle based on excessive consumption and social injustice. For this reason, in many countries, it is recognized that local governments have an important role in dealing with the climate crisis and local climate change plans are being prepared. Ankara has also started to feel the consequences of climate change. Factors such as changing precipitation regimes, drought, floods, and negative impacts on agricultural production have a serious impact on urban life. Thus, it is necessary to control the factors that cause climate change in Ankara and to develop adaptation strategies against climate change. For this reason, it is recommended to prepare an "Ankara Climate Action Plan" under the leadership of Ankara Citizen Council with the contribution of all relevant public and private sectors, civil society stakeholders, universities, scientists, and professional chambers. It is recommended that this action plan be prepared with a participatory approach and that adaptation policies be defined on issues such as the use of water resources, public health, technological and managerial capacity, awareness and efficient resource use. Taking into account the consequences of climate change, and ensuring mitigation in zoning planning and practices, construction principles and layout, green area project design, implementation and maintenance systems, transportation and other emission-generating elements of the capital are also suggested.

This recommendation was approved and entered into force with the decision of the Greater Ankara Municipality Assembly dated November 19, 2019. Following the adoption of this recommendation, Ankara Citizen Council continued to work with the Municipality and the Citizen Council to make progress on this issue and to implement the recommendation. As a result, Greater Ankara Municipality established a Climate Change and Adaptation Branch Directorate under the Department of Environmental Protection and Control to carry out these activities. The "Regulation Amending the Regulation on Norm Staff Principles and Standards for Municipalities and Affiliated Organizations and Local Administrative Unions" published in the Official Gazette dated April 8, 2020, led to the establishment of "Climate Change Department" in metropolitan municipalities and "Climate Change Branch Directorate" in provincial and district municipalities. As of the date of the establishment of the Branch Directorate, only 14 of the 30 Metropolitan Municipalities had a greenhouse gas inventory, 9 of them had a Greenhouse Gas Reduction Target and Action Plan, and 5 of them had an Adaptation Action Plan. Ankara was among the cities without a Greenhouse Gas Inventory.

After the Climate Change and Adaptation Branch Directorate had taken over the work on the Action Plan, a Branch Manager was appointed to the relevant Directorate and a consultancy service was procured from a private sector company for the preparation of the plan. The plan was prepared by a private firm, which won the bid for the preparation of the plan. A stakeholder analysis was conducted at the beginning of the plan preparation and a participatory consultation process was planned. In this context, the plan preparation team held an online workshop with Ankara Citizen council components and received their opinions on the plan on June 15, 2021. The plan was finalized by the end of 2021 and published on Greater Ankara Municipality's website with the following introduction:

> "In line with the changes in Ankara's precipitation data and temperature values as well as national and global projections on climate change, Ankara is expected to face drought and related problems that will arise due to climate change in the medium term. In the IPCC scenario, annual average temperatures in Türkiye will rise by 2.5 - 4 C by 2050 unless necessary measures are taken. It is stated that the south of Türkiye will face serious drought threats, while the risk of flooding will increase in the northern regions. Ankara is also listed among the provinces that will be exposed to drought. Indicators related to climate change in Ankara show that there have been some changes in the long term. Annual average temperature changes are in line with the global temperature increase trend. In addition, according to TURKSTAT's provincial life index (2015) survey results, both air and noise pollution are areas where measures need to be taken for Ankara. Studies have determined

the vulnerability of the city of Ankara to climate change as "highly vulnerable".

As a result of the participatory process and evaluations carried out in the plan within three different development scenarios determined for the development of Ankara for greenhouse gas emissions, it was decided to determine adaptation and mitigation strategies in the following main action areas:

- Open-Green Space and Corridors
- Urban Heat Island Effects
- Urban Streams
- Water Management
- Waste Management
- Land Use
- Agriculture/Forestry, Food Security and Biodiversity
- Transportation and Infrastructure

Immediately after the completion of the plan, the Municipality announced to the public in December 2021 that the "Green City Action Plan" studies were initiated within the scope of the EBRD Green Cities program. It was reported that this study will be carried out by the international firm ARUP. No information has yet been available on how the climate action plan implementation process will be carried out from this stage. However, it is assessed that the issue will be addressed from a broader framework in the green city action plan process. On the other hand, to develop a more effective monitoring process regarding this process within Ankara Citizen Council, the existing Environment and Zero Waste Working Group will be transformed into a "Climate and Environment Council" and to follow the developments in the international arena and to carry out awareness raising activities in Ankara. In this context, the president of Ankara Citizen Council attended the Glasgow Climate Summit. In early 2022, it aims to raise awareness by organizing an international "Eco-Climate Summit" in which all components of Ankara Citizen Council will participate.

İmrahor Vadisi (Imrahor Valley) nature-based strategies project

Today, with more than half of the world's population living in cities, it is becoming increasingly important to protect ecologically sensitive areas in urban areas with nature-based solutions and to ensure the continuity of urban life around them. Although many areas in Ankara are subject to discussion in this sense, the importance of Imrahor Valley, which has come to the fore due to some urban mega-projects that have been highlighted in recent years, has prompted Ankara Citizen Council to make efforts in this regard. A project was submitted to the SGP-GEF (Small Grants Program) of the UNDP together with the

KENTLAB Association to examine similar examples in the world and to reveal the situation in the Imrahor Valley.

With Kent-LAB as project coordinator and Ankara Citizen Council as co-applicant, the project 'Nature-Based Metropolitan Strategies: The Case of Imrahor Valley' project aims to support local governments with nature-based strategies and to protect urban ecosystems and biodiversity by addressing the ecological, sociological, and economic aspects of climate change adaptation in Imrahor Valley of Ankara through participatory processes. Within the scope of the project, 'Ankara Nature-Based Solutions and Conceptual Framework Workshops' were organized to define and evaluate the spatial planning processes in Ankara and Imrahor Valley and to strengthen the technical capacity of civil society organizations by presenting the conceptual framework of legislation, problems, potentials and solution proposals. At the same time, a holistic conceptual framework on nature-based solutions, blue-green infrastructure, urban ecosystem services, etc. was defined and best practices from the world with similar characteristics to Ankara's urban macro form and climate were evaluated. Within the scope of the project, two separate workshops - one online and one hybrid - were organized in October 2021, and early 2022, and the opinions and suggestions of international, national, and local experts and Ankara Citizen Council components were put forward. The reports of the project were published, documenting the current situation and destruction in Imrahor Valley and the approaches agreed upon by the stakeholders. In line with these projects, preparations for implementation projects for the cultivation of endemic species in the area are ongoing.

Covid-19 Pandemic Resilient Cities and Sponge City Press Releases

The Covid-19 Pandemic period was a period in which Ankara Citizen Council, together with the academic staff working in the executive board, working groups, and assemblies, produced various evaluation texts to enlighten the people of Ankara and society. In particular, to understand the effects of the Covid-19 Pandemic on cities, to take the necessary measures on time, and to discuss the right policies for the future, the determinations made based on the concept of resilient cities were shared with the public. With these studies carried out under the coordination of the Vice President of the Citizen Council, the issue was associated with the climate change process, which started to be discussed immediately after the Covid-19 Pandemic. In this context, two important declarations on the principles of Covid-19 Pandemic-resilient cities and flood-resilient cities were shared with the public and attracted wide attention.

8. International Recognition and Awards

In today's world, awards play an important role in determining the level of achievement of an organization's objectives and the effectiveness of its activities and processes. Awards in the field of organizational development not only identify a clear achievement but also contribute to the recognition of the level of organizational development and the documentation of an ongoing development process by an external system. However, the level of institutionalization, sustainability, and continuity of the award itself, as well as how the philosophy of the award is defined, and how it is positioned in terms of contributing to the development of organizational processes rather than declaring a champion, comes to the fore here. Associating volunteer work with award systems may lose the quality of being a tool for increasing the trust and motivation of internal and external stakeholders. However, for an organization to follow the awards in its field, apply for them, and monitor the results is itself a learning and development adventure for institutional development.

Ankara Citizen Council, which joined the Turkish citizen council experience quite late in the process, had an important opportunity to monitor other citizen councils and benefit from their experiences. Since the establishment of the Council, a modeling of the tools and elements of participatory governance was undertaken. The successes achieved with the contribution of "facilitation" approaches one of the important elements of this modeling, formed the starting point for the idea of applying for an award. In other words, the first award received by Ankara Citizen Council was closely related to the participatory approaches it applied within itself.

On June 29, 2019, Ankara Citizen Council held its first general assembly and started to contribute to a truly democratic participatory process in Ankara. The Council's contributions became visible in the unanimous adoption of the recommendations by the Greater Ankara Municipality Assembly and especially in the solidarity organized during the Covid-19 Pandemic period. Moreover, Ankara Citizen Council's contacts with other citizen councils in the country showed that this difference and awareness was at a very high level. In this direction, the aim of interacting with international organizations was evaluated by the Executive Board and it was decided that the developments in this field would be monitored by the Vice President of the Council.

Facilitation Impact Award (FIA) in 2020

Since February 29, 2020, when the 3rd General Assembly of Ankara Citizen Council was held, international programs on democratic participation have started to be examined and evaluated. In the spring of 2020, the call for the "Facilitation Impact Award" of the "International Association of Facilitators" (IAF), of which Ankara Citizen Council is a member, was published. It was considered that applying for this international award could contribute to the recognition of the participation model implemented by Ankara Citizen Council not only in Ankara but also in Türkiye, and to increase the morale and motivation of citizen councils and it was decided to apply for this award. Apart from some limited contacts, citizen councils in Türkiye have not been involved in such an international interaction and preparation process so far.

The International Association of Facilitators (IAF) is an international organization of moderators and facilitators working in 65 countries around the world. Operating since 1994, the organization sets facilitation standards for participatory corporate governance. The Association embraces the principles of inclusiveness, openness, global perspective, professionalism, leadership, and excellence, and advocates the potential of democratic and institutional development through the power of human interaction. As the values and goals of the Association are also embraced by Ankara Citizen Council, it is very valuable to be nominated for an award given by the Association. In particular, the value that the Association places on people-to-people interaction and professionalism in this field was deemed important. With the "Facilitation Impact Awards", IAF supports initiatives that have had a significant impact on the relationships with its stakeholders.

The Facilitation Impact Award is given by a panel of experts to institutions and organizations around the world and the facilitators who support them, taking into account the facilitation methods they use, the level of achievement of their goals in terms of participation, and the creative and innovative methods they use to achieve these goals. Since 2013, the award has been given to universities, local governments, citizen initiatives, well-known private sector companies, and public institutions from many different countries around the world. The requirements for applying for the award include working with an expert facilitator and using participatory approaches in the right way for positive change. The award aims to recognize and promote the human interaction dimension of participation. In terms of the principle of democratic participation, the social interaction, group dynamics, and psychological dimensions of participation are addressed within the scope of these activities.

Ankara Citizen Council applied for the Facilitation Impact Award at the end of June 2020. In the application file prepared by the Vice President information on the founding objectives of the Council, the level of achievement of these objectives, and the facilitation methods used were included. In the application, the level of inclusiveness and participant profile reached by Ankara Citizen Council, the approval of the advisory decisions taken by Greater Ankara Municipality Council, and the efforts made to create the culture and identity of Ankara based on solidarity, especially during the Covid-19 Pandemic period, were expressed.

Each organization was also required to submit a title for the award application. The title chosen by Ankara Citizen Council was "Citizens of Ankara: Re-Assemble". There was an important meaning behind this title. This title was used to express the openness to participation in the process that started with the election of Mansur Yavaş as mayor after 2019 in Ankara, which had been in a state of serious backwardness in terms of democratic participation for many years despite its high level of education and income and being a capital city, also expressed the mission of the citizen council. Ankara Citizen Council had started working to bring together all citizens at the metropolitan level, where no effective citizen council had been established before, and it was appropriate to reflect this in this award application. For this purpose, an English wordplay from the popular culture of the time was used. The cult phrase "Avengers Assemble" from a scene in the well-known comic book movie "Avengers Endgame", released a year before the award, was used in the award application. In a sense, the message was that every Ankara resident who came together to make the award application possible was a hero. This interesting emphasis was also appreciated by IAF officials.

On August 17, 2020, IAF Officials informed the Council that it had been accepted for the award nomination. It was reported that the award ceremony will take place virtually due to the Covid-19 Pandemic. Since Ankara Citizen Council was nominated for such a valuable award, the nomination was shared with the public through the Council's social media accounts and was widely covered in the press.

For the organization of the award process, IAF Officials held a Zoom meeting on October 7, 2020, with representatives of all nominated institutions and organizations. In this meeting, details of the announcement and dissemination of the award were discussed. It was stated that the institutions and organizations nominated for the award were announced on the IAF website, but the platinum, gold, and silver award categories will be announced at the award night to be held on October 26, 2020. President and Vice President attended the meeting on behalf of Ankara Citizen Council. After this meeting, the Executive Committee was informed as it was now certain that there would be an award, and the organization of the award night was discussed. An approach was adopted where Ankara Citizen Council components would watch the live broadcast together on the award night. IAF also requested a one-minute video promoting the nomination of Ankara Citizen Council to promote the award on social media platforms. The video, written and produced by the Vice President of the Council, was published on IAF and Ankara Citizen Council social media channels. The video was the most viewed of all the videos shared by the IAF to date. The impact of the video, which has been viewed over thirty thousand times, was also appreciated by IAF officials.

Due to the Covid-19 Pandemic conditions, IAF announced that an award ceremony would be organized live on the Internet under the management of a board member. For all components of the citizen council to share this joy, an arrangement was made in Ankara Citizen Council building where a limited number of participants could watch the live broadcast. As there would be a connection to Ankara at some stage of the live broadcast, the IAF was informed about this organization, and this initiative was welcomed. Greater Ankara Municipality and Citizen Council officials, Ankara Citizen Council Executive Board members, Working Group, and Assembly spokespersons participated in the event where the live broadcast would be watched jointly. The program started on 26 October 2022 at 18:00 Turkish time. Participation in the live broadcast was also shared publicly on all social media platforms and simultaneous translation was provided for those in the hall.

At the opening of the program, information about the award was presented. Then the Facilitation Impact Award, silver, gold, and platinum awards were announced respectively. Each award category was presented by an IAF representative from a different country in the world. The excitement peaked in the gold award category presented by Rachel Song-Yeon Kim, South Korean representative and IAF Board Member, and it was announced that Ankara Citizen Council was deemed worthy of the gold medal. Ankara Citizen Council received an institutional award where the Vice President Prof. Dr. Savaş Zafer Şahin received an individual award for his role as a facilitator in the process, thus Ankara received two awards at the end.

Ankara Citizen Council was the first organization from Türkiye to receive this award, and the first metropolitan citizen council to receive such an international award. Apart from Ankara, 16 institutions and organizations from 10 countries were found worthy of the award. It was also noteworthy that Ankara Citizen Council was the only organization among these institutions that was active in the field of participation in city governance. The award night was watched by more than a thousand experts from all over the world, and videos about the award were viewed nearly a hundred thousand times.

The Participation Impact Award is expected to bring significant benefits to Türkiye and Ankara. First, it will increase Türkiye's reputation for local democracy around the world and will be the subject of international research. The number of international organizations reaching out to Ankara Citizen Council after this award has increased, paving the way for further award applications. During the award evaluation process, experts from the Balkans, Europe, and Southeast Asia started contacts to listen to the experience of Ankara Citizen Council. In addition to sharing Ankara's experience, the capital city has now gained the right to participate in international platforms in this field, as well as the advantage to benefit from project and research funding. This is the first time that a citizen council from Türkiye has received such an award, which will help citizen councils to be taken more seriously by local governments. Above all, it is hoped that such an award for Ankara, which does not have a good record in terms of participation, will be a source of pride for the people of Ankara, and that the idea that participation will start to lead to a rethinking of the city's identity and culture.

The international facilitation impact award given to Ankara Citizen Council has also increased the motivation and commitment of the stakeholders within the Citizen Council and contributed to the development of empathy between the components. Many components of the Citizen Council expressed their happiness and satisfaction with the award on social media, WhatsApp, and other platforms. The award was also appreciated by citizen councils of districts in Ankara. After the award, the number of members of Ankara Citizen Council increased, and the perception that there was something new and different about Ankara Citizen Council, apart from the known work and models of citizen councils, increased throughout Türkiye. However, after receiving this award, no other institution or organization in Türkiye has applied for the same award, nor has it attempted to benefit from the experience of Ankara Citizen Council. This can be considered a consequence of the low level of awareness of these issues in Türkiye. On the other hand, it is pleasing to note that IAF and the Istanbul Branch's relationship with Ankara Citizen Council continues to strengthen and joint projects are being carried out.

OIDP Best Practice in Citizen Participation Award in 2021

Following Ankara Citizen Council's receipt of IAF's Facilitation Impact Award in 2020, the Citizen Council started to receive calls for international cooperation and partnership opportunities, especially from IAF contacts. One of these calls was made by the International Observatory for Participatory Democracy (IOPD) created by the United Cities and Local Governments of the World (UCLG). IOPD is an international network open to all cities, organizations, and research centers interested in learning, collaborating, and implementing participatory democracy experiences at the local level. It was established in 2001 within the framework of the European Commission's URB-AL program for decentralized cooperation and was officially launched in Barcelona in November 2001, during the First IOPD Conference. It has also been working with the United Cities and Local Governments (UCLG) since 2006. The network organizes working groups and conferences and awards a prize for participatory democracy every year. The network which closely monitors structures such as participatory budgeting and citizen associations working in the field of participatory democracy prepares annual reports and shares them with its members.

Having been informed about IOPD's activities, the Executive Committee of Ankara Citizen Council applied for membership to the network at the beginning of 2021. The membership application was approved by IOPD's Coordination Committee on April 22, 2021. After reviewing the membership application file, the Committee invited the Citizen Council to apply for the 2021 Best Practice in Citizen Participation Award. Since then, Ankara Citizen Council has been included in the IOPD information network as an associate member.

The IOPD Award for "Best Practice in Citizen Participation" is an initiative launched by the International Observatory for Participatory Democracy (IOPD). The Award is open to all cities and local governments around the world, as well as associations, organizations, and research centers that want to learn about participatory democracy, share their experiences, and implement participatory democracy experiences at the local level. The awarding of this Prize aims to encourage the implementation of innovative experiences at the local level, to expand practices that promote participation, as well as to familiarize interested citizens with the processes involved in the elaboration and implementation of public policies. Furthermore, the aim is to give visibility to these practices in a more direct way, to bring them to the attention of other local authorities so that they can be replicated, and to foster networking. In 2021, the prize was awarded for the 15th time.

In the evaluation of the Award, local initiatives that have set the following objectives for themselves will be considered:

- Developing a benchmark for achieving higher levels of equity in terms of participation and inclusion of diversity
- Empowering citizens who cannot organize to empower the community.
- Increasing citizens' rights in terms of political participation
- Linking different means of participation within a participatory democracy "ecosystem"
- Improving the quality of public decision-making through participatory mechanisms
- Increasing the effectiveness and efficiency of participatory democracy mechanisms
- Improve the evaluation and monitoring of participatory democracy mechanisms.

The Award envisages a five-stage evaluation. In 2021, for the first time, due to the Covid-19 Pandemic, all stages of the evaluation were conducted virtually. In the first stage, candidates send their application proposals to IOPD. The application form can be submitted in English, Spanish,

French, and Portuguese, along with the required visual and written attachments. In the second stage, the IOPD secretariat evaluates the application for compliance with the general conditions. In the third stage, the information of the applicants is published on a digital platform and both the candidates and anyone who wishes to support them can support them by voting and commenting. The 20 candidates with the most comments and votes are expected to advance to the next round. In the fourth stage, each member of the international Jury evaluates the 10 candidates submitted to them and prepares a report. In addition to the most successful candidate, the jury has the right to determine five special awards. The jury's evaluation criteria are the level of innovation, replicability or transferability, level of feasibility, the level of planning and coordination, and the level of shared responsibility. Stakeholders contributing to the process, mechanisms for evaluating results, and stakeholder accountability for competencies, and style, accuracy, and conciseness of the application are also taken into consideration. In the fifth stage, the selected awardees are announced during IOPD's annual conference, with the evaluation reports forwarded to the nominees.

The application for the award was submitted on April 30, 2021, by the Vice President of the Citizen Council, as the contact person with the authority granted by the Executive Board of Ankara Citizen Council. In the application file, information on the founding objectives of the Council, the extent to which these objectives have been achieved, and the participation methods used were included. The purpose of Ankara Citizen Council is stated in the application as follows:

"Our goal is to achieve higher levels of equality in terms of citizen participation and to recognize diversity as an element of inclusion. This is because in Ankara, the capital of Türkiye, nearly six million people live in a vast metropolitan area in Central Anatolia that is highly politically polarized due to the twenty-five-year reign of a previous mayor known for his autocratic, nepotistic and corrupt administration that eroded community awareness and participatory practices. The challenge is to establish an inclusive, credible, and well-organized participatory mechanism to bring together citizens and diverse stakeholders in Ankara".

In the application, Ankara Citizen Council is introduced as an autonomous and participatory organization established to consolidate community engagement efforts and citizen initiatives at the street, neighborhood, district, and metropolitan levels to define key urban policies and raise public awareness on sustainable development, livability, and good governance. The objectives of the Citizen Council are presented as; (1) Convincing a significant number of stakeholders in Ankara to join Ankara Citizen

Council and gaining their trust (2) Defining local policies and strategies to address Ankara's structural problems with the members of the Citizen council and ensuring that these proposals are accepted by the Metropolitan Municipality (3) Strengthening the City Identity and creating concrete examples of solidarity among citizens, especially in emergencies. The application also detailed how many of these objectives have been achieved in two years and through which innovative methods. The previous IAF Facilitation Impact Award was also mentioned.

The IOPD Best Practice in Citizen Participation Award received over a hundred nominations from the public, of which 52 made it to the second round. Among the accepted candidates, there were nominees from many regions of the world and Türkiye. However, only Ankara Citizen Council appeared to be a fully participatory organization without the involvement of any local government unit. The candidates were voted for other candidates and external participants through a digital platform. At the end of the voting, Ankara Citizen Council came first with 1202 votes. Nearly twenty thousand experts from around the world participated in the entire voting process. At the end of the voting, all candidates were announced in the IOPD international database for experience sharing. It was decided that the 26 candidates with the highest number of votes would proceed to the third round.

In July 2021, the award jury started the evaluation of these 26 nominees, and five of them were selected for the award. After the Jury prepared their evaluation reports, a special interview was conducted with each finalist candidate. During this evaluation process, the Vice President had a successful interview with Prof. Yvet Cabannes, a renowned development expert and lecturer at the University of London, one of the IOPD Secretariat and Jury members, on October 14, 2021. During the interview, the experience of Ankara Citizen Council was evaluated in terms of gender equality, accountability, monitoring and evaluation mechanisms, and experience transfer in participation. All these interviews were then published online by IOPD. After these stages, Ankara Citizen Council was officially notified that it was awarded one of the Jury Special Awards for Best Practice in Citizen Participation 2021. The award was announced at the United Cities and Local Governments Summit on October 17th and disseminated on social media platforms. Previously, there were municipalities from Türkiye that received this award in the field of local government. Ankara Citizen Council was the first citizen council from Türkiye to receive this award. In addition to Ankara Citizen Council, the city governments of Mexico, Gothenburg, Milan, and Rio de Janeiro also received the special award. The award to Ankara Citizen Council was widely covered by the national and local press. The award was announced at the opening ceremony of the 3rd Citizen Councils Symposium held in Balıkesir between October

18-21, 2021, in cooperation with the Union of Citizen Councils of Türkiye and Balıkesir Citizen Council.

The special award for the best practice in citizen participation given to Ankara Citizen Council contributed to the transformation of the award process into a collective process by enabling stakeholders within the Citizen Council to follow and participate in the award process. Many components of the Citizen Council expressed their happiness and satisfaction with the award on platforms such as social media and WhatsApp. The number of members of Ankara Citizen Council increased after the award, and the perception of Ankara Citizen Council as a reference for citizen councils across Türkiye has improved. However, even after receiving this award, no other institution or organization in Türkiye has taken the initiative to benefit from the experience of Ankara Citizen Council on this issue. This can be considered a consequence of the low level of awareness of these issues in Türkiye. On the other hand, gratifyingly, the impact of the award within the IOPD community continues and interaction is flourishing.

2021 INTERNATIONAL OBSERVATORY ON PARTICIPATORY DEMOCRACY
15th AWARD
BEST PRACTICE
IN CITIZEN
PARTICIPATION
The International Observatory of Participatory Democracy
recognizes with a special mention
Ankara Metropolitan Municipality
for the experience
The Citizens' Assembly of Ankara
Marc Serra Solé
IOPD Secretary General
IOPD
UCLG

9. Conclusion

Democracy and citizens' involvement in decision-making processes with participatory approaches are among the areas where humanity hopes to make progress in the 21st century. It is increasingly argued that many problem areas; from the climate crisis to mitigating the negative effects of rapid progress in disruptive technologies, from mass migrations to regional conflicts, can only be permanently resolved in this way. For this reason, many countries and societies from the global south and north are striving to develop practices that claim to be effective for inclusivity, participation and good governance both at the community scale and in large settlements. In this quest, unique examples, mostly driven by civil initiatives and non-profit social innovation initiatives, interact with each other on an international scale and build a rich learning process. For this reason, it is important to share and explain cases of good practices in this area for further progress.

The emergence of this need is closely related to the decline in democratic representation and the accompanying rise of authoritarian populist regimes. While in many countries leaders who remain in power for a long time and are equipped with excessive powers no longer leave room for democracy to develop, the increasing demand for participatory democracy all over the world suggests a need for transformation. Although the stronger expression of demands for participation and good governance in Western democracies set an ideal, what has been achieved by examples in countries where these demands are more difficult to express gives more hope for a democratic culture. For this reason, this book aims to explain such an example in detail.

Contrary to the popular belief, it is a frequently expressed fact that Türkiye, which is at a transition point between continents and cultures, exhibits unique examples of democracy. Türkiye has been adopting good governance and participatory democracy for a long time and has been practicing in this regard. In addition to being a requirement of the membership process of the European Union and international agreements, Türkiye's long state and modernization adventure pushes to make efforts in this regard. Although the tense processes between localization and centralization rarely allow structural transformations due to fragile issues such as religion, ethnic identities, terrorism, and international migration, interesting examples can be encountered in the field of participatory democracy. Ankara Citizen Council, which is the subject of this book, has created a very exciting experience in this sense.

Unlike the "citizen assembly" type organizations observed in many countries of the world in the last twenty years and designed for citizens to directly participate in the decision-making process, participatory democracy in Türkiye is still shaped through permanent associations of institutionalized civil society and public and private sector members. For this purpose, participatory platforms called citizen councils have existed as a part of municipal law since the 2000s. Citizen councils, as one of the unique examples in the field of democratic participation, have long pointed to a potential for citizens to participate in government. Established for the participation of citizens in city management on issues such as sustainable development, urban identity, city vision, and good governance, these structures have set good examples over time and have maintained their feature as the only official participatory mechanism at the local level. In a country where the participation of citizens is way behind expected levels, citizen councils represent a significant opportunity.

After twenty years of experience, the citizen council established in the capital has emerged as an internationally recognized platform for democratic participation, hosting successful experiences in solidarity, good governance, and addressing many other issues. The realization of this experience in Ankara, which had been governed by an administration that was against citizen participation for the last twenty-five years, has been a source of hope for other city councils and participatory efforts in the country. In fact, at a time when polarization and conflicts between the central government and opposition municipalities in local governments were very visible, Ankara City Council showed that very different segments of the society could come together with the right policy approach and handle urban issues with consensus. Ankara, nourished by different city council experiences in different geographies of Türkiye, has achieved many successful results by implementing an innovative and well-studied participation model. The use of the right facilitation methods in participation together with a thorough institutionalization approach were at the core of this model.

Although there were political, bureaucratic and cultural obstacles during the process, Ankara Citizen Council managed to bring together 1800 institutional representatives and over 5000 citizens in the city to effectively address city's problems and discuss policy alternatives. Although politicians perceive effective participation as a serious threat, bureaucrats do not want to share the policy-making space, the right cultural codes and behavioral patterns for participation are lacking in general, intensive efforts have been made to make the city council an effective participation platform in Ankara. The constituents of the Citizen Council were brought together in working groups and assemblies to mobilize civil society around urban problems of Ankara. This resulted in awareness-raising events, projects and programs related to urban identity, memory, urban space, environmental issues, quality of life, community engagement and solidarity in times of crisis.

As a result, Ankara Citizen Council has become an institutionally accepted participatory mechanism and seen as credible by its members and citizens. The work carried out within this mechanism was submitted to the municipal council in the form of more than a hundred recommendations and was approved unanimously. As a result of the efforts spent to institutionalize the general structure of the city council, an effective and inviting administrative process in which citizens can participate has emerged. With this decision-making structure, alternative methods such as competitions reviving the city's memory and identity elements were held, proposals were developed for the transformation of public spaces and conservation of historical areas, and efforts were made to enhance the urban aesthetics. Studies on participatory budgeting, gender equality and the effective participation of vulnerable groups - youth, disabled people, elderly people and children - starting from the neighborhood level were carried out. Events were organized to share academic and expert opinions on urban issues such as transportation, housing, livelihood, environmental problems and quality of life. During the Covid-19 Pandemic, floods, fires and earthquakes, exemplary solidarity campaigns were organized not only in Ankara but throughout Türkiye.

Visibility and widespread impact were also taken into consideration and communication and media tools were effectively used to make the participatory process more effective. These studies have led to the formation of a partnership based on a culture of cooperation and working together between the city council, the municipality and other public institutions. These achievements have been recognized with awards not only in Türkiye but also internationally.

Undoubtedly, the issue of the future and resilience of Ankara Citizen Council example is also discussed considering the results of this meaningful experience. The legislation of the city council, which allows institutionalization but leaves the continuity of the citizen councils to the will of the mayors, creates doubts about the future of Ankara Citizen Council. However, this obstacle can be overcome if the citizen council experience has led to public awareness and individuals involved in the council processes created a sufficiently resilient structure. Although the experience shows that the city council is embraced in Ankara, the route the city council will follow in the next term will be determined especially by the dynamics of the 2024 local elections in Türkiye.

Afterword

Aliye Pekin Çelik

"Cities are engines of economic growth and innovation that hold the key to achieving the 2030 Agenda and the Sustainable Development Goals. They are also on the frontlines of today's complex challenges, from the climate crisis to growing inequalities and political polarization. But local authorities are struggling with limited support and resources, while demand for infrastructure, affordable housing, efficient transport, and social services is immense and growing." These are the words of the Secretary General of the United Nations at the 2023 Financing Sustainable Urban Development meeting.

By the 21st century the UN Delegations were interested to achieve sustainable development through local governments as much as national governments all over the world. It became obvious that state's efforts are not enough to reduce poverty. Member states started to focus on "Effective governance, policy making and planning for sustainable development."

Thus the concept of "urban governance" became very important as the role of community participation and inclusive, transparent policies were proven effective.

Participatory And Resilient Urban Governance, The Case of Ankara Citizen Council demonstrates a great example of a successful practice that would be replicable in other parts of the world where the fast growing population in cities will be 73 % by 2050. Local Governments have social, political economic and environmental difficulties. Improvement of the urban governance models through participatory governance has become very important for achieving sustainable cities as mentioned at UN reports, the SG's speeches, United Cities and Local Governments (UCLG) and the Global Task Force reports. This book has the power to prove it by example.

APPENDICES

I. Advisory Decision titles of Ankara Citizen Council Presented to the Municipal Council in 2023[11]

1) Sakarya battlefield live-action activities
2) Support for the capital Ankara's 100th anniversary half marathon, 10k run
3) Book/100 photos 100 stories for the meaningful events of the war of independence on the 100th anniversary of Ankara becoming the capital and the republic
4) Making a documentary on the roads opening to the republic: supporting the production of a documentary about the important roads from İnebolu to İzmir in the War of Independence
5) Revealing the values of Ankara from past to present through the eyes of a photographer on the 100th anniversary of Ankara becoming the capital by a photo safari
6) Independence flag on the way to the republic project, with events to be held in Ankara on the 100th anniversary
7) Mapping work at Ankara castle gate on important days for the War of Independence and the republic.
8) Faces of young people on the 100th-anniversary project: collecting and publishing the opinions of 100 young people from different disciplines on the republic in the 100th anniversary of the republic with short videos
9) Supporting the resurrection road march, which was previously held in Sakarya village, as a larger event with the 100th anniversary theme
10) Inviting Ned Pamphilon, whose work titled Atatürk's Eyes is exhibited in Anitkabir, to carry out 100th-anniversary activities with him

[11] These recommendations were all approved by the Municipal Council unanimously in October 2023.

11) Supporting the production of a documentary telling the stories of the 1st parliament building, 2-direction building, 3-maliköy train station, 4-çoban school, 5-alagöz commander-in-chief headquarters and 6-Abidin pasha mansion, which are the 6 important buildings that witnessed the 100th anniversary of the republic from liberation to the establishment.
12) Applying discounted public transport and parking tariffs to passengers using bicycles in transportation
13) Establishing a bicycle velodrome at international standards in Ankara
14) Providing financial support to cycling sports clubs and establishing Ankara cycling team
15) Encouraging bicycle production in Ankara, establishing bicycle spare parts and repair stations, and cooperating with professional chambers and organized industrial estates for this purpose
16) Development and dissemination of an electric bicycle-sharing system
17) Establishment of bicycle parking areas in all public institution buildings, public areas, and Greater Ankara Municipality service buildings in Ankara, integrated with bicycle paths and public transportation
18) Taking necessary precautions on issues such as traffic signs, warning signs, night lighting, and road infrastructure to make the existing transportation system suitable for bicycle transportation.
19) Organizing a public relations campaign to explain to the public that bicycle transportation is a safe mode of transportation
20) Taking necessary precautions for women, youth, disabled people and all disadvantaged individuals to participate in bicycle transportation in Ankara
21) Taking necessary precautions to effectively consider the bicycle element in transportation planning studies in Ankara
22) Ensuring the participation of Ankara City Council bicycle assembly in UKOME meetings with observer status on issues regarding bicycle infrastructure and its use in Ankara
23) Providing continuous training to the public and municipal employees on bicycle use and increasing the population trained in bicycle transportation

24) Arrangement of working conditions to incentivize municipal employees to come from home to work by bicycle (shower and locker facilities, incentive bonuses, etc.)
25) Expansion of bicycle transport devices, which have started to be placed in public vehicles, throughout the entire public transportation system
26) Providing bicycle integration to the park-and-ride system established in Ankara and providing advantageous conditions to users who will continue by bicycle
27) Providing free bicycles to families who can use bicycle transportation to encourage families to whom the municipality provides social assistance to use bicycle transportation.
28) Starting a campaign to recycle scrap bicycles and provide new bicycles to those who bring unusable bicycles
29) Organizing regular annual bicycle workshops to bring together all stakeholders regarding bicycle use in Ankara
30) Regularly sharing all data regarding bicycle use in Ankara with the public from the open-source database of the municipality
31) Review of institutional possibilities for transforming municipal disability services and rehabilitation branch directorate into a department headquarters
32) 1st Ankara barrier-free life fair and conference
33) Support for special individuals in mixed children's choir
34) Participation of disabled individuals in production
35) Expanding the scope of respite houses
36) Cooperation platform to solve the housing crisis
37) Conducting a study on how to create a youth policies action plan and implement it together with the municipal organization chart
38) In order for Ankara to become a brand in the field of youth, it is recommended to show interest in the title of European youth capital, which is given every year by the European Youth Forum, and to take steps to fulfill the necessary conditions for Ankara to receive this title.
39) We recommend that Ankara develops student-friendly approaches and increases the number of municipal youth centers to ensure that young people create value for the city and that a new generation participation model be built in these centers.

40) Hold monthly council meetings open to youth in cooperation with the capital youth council to instantly identify the different problems and needs of university students studying in the capital Ankara.

41) Supporting cooperatives, small producers, and family farming

42) Supporting the project management process of cooperatives and small producers and providing technical and mentoring support

43) Establishment of compost production system on Ankara scale

44) Strategic planning to create the required capacity to develop non-agricultural production activities in rural areas

45) Preparation of a master plan to eliminate irrigation problems resulting from climate change and regional geographic problems in rural Ankara

46) Organizing the 100th-anniversary summit of cooperatives on the 100th anniversary of Ankara becoming the capital.

47) Development of participatory rural area management models to support rural development in rural Ankara with the participation of village headmen and cooperatives

48) Improving the urban aesthetics and increasing the visibility of the capital

49) Organizing an "art season-opening event" to promote all national and international cultural and artistic activities to be held in the capital Ankara every September.

50) Arranging "micro activity areas" in existing and new parking areas in Ankara and providing free use to workers carrying out culture and art activities

51) Non-governmental organizations operating in the field of culture and arts in Ankara center will be located in a building to be allocated by the municipality, using common areas together, and increasing both experiences sharing and business development opportunities with a cluster model.

52) Preparation of Atatürk Forest farm action plan

53) Preparation of an action plan for the protection of modern heritage

54) Creating a competition action plan in Ankara

55) Defense system against climate change: detection and mapping of the threats caused by Ankara zoning regulation and applications in the context of adaptation to climate change

56) Urban and natural environment; action plan to protect and maintain cultural and ecological landscape values

57)Creating a “crowd-design platform" where professionals who want to contribute design to the capital Ankara can exhibit their products.
58)Reconstruction and revitalization of the previously demolished dam casino, located in the Çubuk dam recreation area, and the demolished water filter building, located in Etlik, with a culture and art function.
59)Identification of districts and neighborhoods in Ankara with historical depth and spatial integrity, together with their tangible and intangible cultural heritage, and creating an inventory
60)Re-evaluation of public hospitals located in the city center of Ankara by the municipality for the provision of emergency health services and social services.
61)Recommendation on method suggestion on naming public areas (avenue-street-park)
62)Organizing an ancestral seeds exchange festival to include farmers and producers in Ankara rural area
63)Production of natural vegetation species (hawthorn, pear, blueberry and similar species) of Ankara and central Anatolia region, propagation and dissemination in all urban living areas, parks
64)Carrying out studies to disseminate the studies carried out by rural producers to produce products such as herbaceous plants, bulbous plants, shrubs and trees that can be used in the design processes in urban parks, throughout Ankara rural area, especially women should be included in these processes.
65)Taking the necessary steps to uncover Ankara's streams by opening a certain part of the İncesu stream, which is identified with Ankara and the source of inspiration for poems, folk songs and songs. Recreational planning/design of this section of İncesu stream exposed to the surface.
66)Reconsidering the İmrahor Valley following nature-based and ecological approaches and reconsidering the development plans to protect aquatic and terrestrial diversity.
67)Reviewing planning approaches that open valley bottoms to development, developing urban transformation approaches to clear the valleys opened to construction.
68)Urban living areas are selected as pilots, preventing and controlling the mixing of sewage, wastewater and rainwater with streams and streams, and integrating with water harvesting studies.

69) Bye-bye grass project: expanding the use of low water requiring, groundcover, herbaceous, shrub and tree species, starting from urban parks.

70) Designing an eco-recreation facility. Sample area: designing idle facilities around Kesikköprü dam and close to Bala - Kesikköprü village within the framework of ecological principles.

71) To restore the old avenues and streets of Ankara, which was once known as the 'city of acacias', mimosa trees, identified with women's struggle and elegance, are produced together with acacia trees and planted in green areas, parks and gardens.

72) Establishing an education and information work program within the scope of disaster preparedness, water literacy and carbon footprint studies, revealing Ankara's carbon preventive capacity, and initiating non-formal education mobilization for the prevention of climate change.

73) Determining the disaster resilience status of building stock in Ankara, starting from all public buildings, and declaring it to the public

74) The first water facilities of the republic, particularly the Atpazarı, Çankaya, Bedesten water tanks and Kırkgöz underground water facility, which can serve Ankara with various new functions with their lifespan of nearly 100 years, should be immediately taken under protection and necessary works should be initiated to transfer them to future generations.

75) To ensure the integration of green belt afforestation works, which have been continued in the nearby Ankara since the 1970s, with urban green areas, and to maintain and develop afforestation activities that will be carried out in solidarity with civil society for this purpose

76) Conducting a master plan study to expand the use of rainwater harvesting and gray water in Ankara. Identifying Ankara's underground and surface water resources, mapping water resources within the scope of the 'blue infrastructure project', and revealing the water use potential.

77) Creating an inventory to identify and protect all trees on the streets and avenues of Ankara with participatory methods.

78) Organizing a workshop and panel series on "circular economy", one of the important discussion topics of the recent period, with the participation of experts and relevant stakeholders

79)Restoring two exemplary village school buildings located in rural settlements neighboring areas with high biodiversity, such as important plant areas, important bird areas, and important nature areas, and creating environments in which education on rural-nature processes is provided.

80)In the case of water scarcity caused by drought and climate change, the protection of water quality is as important as the amount of existing water bodies, and even more important than that. The most important danger of stagnant water bodies, in particular, is the blue-green algae occurring in the water. Known as water algae. Cyanobacteria, especially those with toxic effects, both threaten health and cause rapid deterioration of water quality. Taking measures to control algae production in stagnant waters.

81)Implementing smart energy city procedures.

82)Supporting the making of liaison and cooperation agreements with participatory structures similar to Ankara City Council in cities with which the capital Ankara has sister city agreements.

83)Conducting managerial studies to determine at least 5% of the budgets created in the budget processes of all municipalities in Ankara with the "participatory budgeting" approach, and considering participatory budget studies separately in the evaluation of activity reports

84)Creating a "participation master plan" that will determine all the necessary studies for the development of local democratic participation in the capital Ankara, will be prepared by participatory methods and with the participation of the existing city councils, and will cover all provincial borders.

85)Although the establishment of a city council is a mandatory provision given to the mayors according to article 76 of the municipality law, the city council has not yet been established or the continuity of its former establishment has not been ensured in Mamak, Altındağ, Sincan, Ayaş, Bala, Çamlıdere, Elmadağ, Güdül, Haymana, Kalecik, Nallıhan, Kızılcahamam. Strengthening the establishment and institutionalization process of city councils in the districts and establishing 25 city councils in 25 districts of Ankara.

86)Implementing the "participation project support program" to develop innovative examples of democratic participation in the capital

Ankara and supporting events and activities related to participation financially and in kind.

87)Organizing a project market event with the support of Ankara city council to increase the number and improve the content of joint R&D projects with universities located in the capital Ankara on the development of local services in the city

88)Establishment of "Ankara planning and innovation agency" to increase the project capacity of Greater Ankara Municipality and all district municipalities

89)Greater Ankara Municipality should launch a mutual aid website that will enable the increase of scholarship capacity for students in all areas of education and training and support a public relations campaign for this purpose.

90)Establishing a "disaster adaptation and living center" to meet the needs of our citizens who move to the capital Ankara or reside temporarily during disasters and to facilitate the adaptation process to the city

91)Organizing sector workshops to identify the problems of developing economic sectors in the capital Ankara and to improve the services of local governments in this direction

92)Conducting commercial sector analyses and preparing commercial function planning regulations to support the effective and efficient operation of enterprises from different sectors in sub-centers formed in ulus, Kızılay and districts in the capital Ankara.

93)Establishment of a site management organization by law no. 2863 on the protection of cultural and natural assets in the places of Ankara's UNESCO World Heritage sites and historical city centers

94)Bringing together the management of all public and private museums in Ankara and creating the "Ankara museums platform" and receiving support from this platform for municipal activities regarding museums.

95)Preparation of urban design projects of places, streets, avenues and public spaces mentioned in literary works that give Ankara its identity

96)Educational and learning materials should be developed and distributed to schools to make it easier to explain the historical and cultural values of the capital Ankara to children and young people

97)Annual "public health assessment workshops " to improve public health in the capital Ankara

98)Ensuring that Greater Ankara Municipality staff receive training on participation issues from experts
99)Establishing a voluntary legal support system in cooperation with Ankara Bar Association to receive legal support for disadvantaged groups living in Ankara
100) Annual disaster councils should be convened to determine the disaster situation of the capital Ankara, and the disaster resilience of the city should be followed by creating council reports.
101) A neighborhood volunteering system should be established to organize the solidarity force in Ankara after disasters that may occur in different regions of Türkiye.
102) A "disaster solidarity strategic plan" should be prepared to organize the solidarity force in Ankara after disasters that may occur in different regions of Türkiye, and this plan should be shared with all Ankara residents.
103) Preparation of Ankara brand city action research and action plan
104) Supporting existing virtual promotion platforms to activate the tourism potential of the capital Ankara and improving promotion and public relations processes in foreign languages in the city, especially in the historical city center.
105) Organizing a scenario and film competition to promote the events including the process from the war of independence to the establishment of the republic at the international level, in cooperation with all provinces where our war of independence took place
106) Completion of pet cemetery (Melekler Village) establishment works
107) Advisory board: creating an academic support mechanism on policies regarding design in the city by establishing the urban aesthetics and design supreme board
108) Supporting all branches of amateur sports activities in Ankara
109) Establishing an administrative unit at the department level within the Greater Ankara Municipality to provide education-oriented services for problem areas and solution suggestions.
110) Preparation and dissemination of scientific publications and promotional materials to introduce the historical personality of Hacı Bayram-ı Veli to the people of Ankara

II. Relief Efforts of Ankara Citizen Council after the Kahramanmaraş Earthquake

<u>Solidarity Activities Targeting the Earthquake Region:</u>

• Immediately after the news about the devastating power and extent of the earthquake was confirmed, members of the Capital City Youth Assembly and other components of Ankara Citizen Council met with representatives of Çankaya Citizen Council at Ankara Citizen Council building and made an assessment and solidarity strategies were determined.

• Accordingly, first, President of Ankara Citizen Council, moved to the earthquake zone on February 7, 2023, and started to transfer information from the field.

• Secondly, members of the Capital City Youth Assembly established a solidarity center at Ankara Citizen Council Building on the morning of February 7, 2023. In this solidarity center, a communication network of volunteers was established, and the needs of earthquake victims were identified through social media and open-source data.

• On the same day, Ankara Citizen Council components established a communication network for the procurement of materials needed in the earthquake zone.

• Through the established communication network, one-to-one communication was established, and calls were started to address the needs of the earthquake zone. While these calls were being made, hundreds of non-governmental organizations, companies, and volunteer Ankara residents joined this network and started to bring their aid to Ankara Citizen Council.

• Simultaneously, many civil society and professional organizations that are members of Ankara Citizen Council started and carried out similar fundraising processes in liaison with the Council.

• The needs of the earthquake zone and the needs of the earthquake victims who came to Ankara were determined instantaneously through the communication network formed by the members of the Capital City Youth Assembly, and calls were constantly made through social media and other communication channels to meet these needs.

• Solidarity-minded citizens, companies, and non-governmental organizations of the capital city of Ankara individually or institutionally delivered relief supplies to Ankara Citizen Council, and these supplies were carried to the Council building with a human chain by volunteer young people who responded to the call of the Capital City Youth Assembly.
• Since the first days of the earthquake a total of 3000 Ankara Citizen Council volunteers, including 1900 young people, have been continuously involved in these activities.
• All aid materials received by Ankara Citizen Council were carefully classified by the Capital City Youth Assembly and accompanying volunteers, taking into account variables such as age, gender, and urgency, as new, second-hand, and consumer goods, packed in a way not to get wet, and made ready for shipment by writing the contents of the parcel on them and adding solidarity notes.
• A total of 950 tons of material, organized in stations, was sorted and boxed.
• From the first day following the earthquake, supplies started to be sent to the earthquake zone from Ankara Citizen Council building.
• Within approximately two weeks until 19.02.2023, 714 tons of earthquake materials were sent from Ankara Citizen Council building to the earthquake zone in 44 separate vehicles.
• Along with these vehicles, the materials sent to the earthquake zone range from generators to food, hygiene, clothing, and electronic equipment.
• In addition, 166 separate trips were organized from the earthquake zones to Ankara, supporting the access of earthquake victims to Ankara.
• 100 voluntary health and search and rescue personnel were provided with vehicles and sent to the earthquake zone.
• With the established communication network, open-source data was instantly confirmed and shared with AFAD, and support was provided to those in need both in the earthquake zone and Ankara. In this communication operation managed by the Capital City Youth Assembly, around 5,000 young people are supported through different communication channels. As a result of this communication operation:
• After confirming the data obtained from open sources, about 8,000 calls for assistance were added to the AFAD system.

• Approximately 550 young people whose families are in the earthquake zone but who live in Ankara were reached and their needs were identified.
• Communication was established with 3623 earthquake victims trapped under rubble in the earthquake zone, and AFAD and relevant institutions were contacted to help them receive assistance and support their evacuation.
• 3 children and 8 adults under the rubble were rescued.
• 4,000 messages of help and support were verified and presented to social media, and 2,000 accurate information posts were published.

Solidarity activities for earthquake victims arriving in Ankara:

• Ankara Citizen Council initiated a solidarity process to meet the needs of the earthquake victims who came to Ankara by their means, starting from the third day of the earthquake, to provide shelter and necessities.
• With the solidarity of the Executive Board, Working Groups and Assemblies of Ankara Citizen Council, members of Ankara Chamber of Commerce, and mukhtars, the temporary shelter needs of nearly 2000 families and a total of approximately 15000 people have been met so far.
• For this purpose, hotels, dormitories, and vacant and second homes in Ankara and surrounding districts were allocated by benefactors.
• The furniture needs of the earthquake victims, whose shelter needs were met in houses, were met with new and second-hand goods provided by Ankara Citizen Council components from donors.
• From the third day of the earthquake, an aid store was set up in the exhibition hall of Ankara Citizen Council and the Council started to provide the earthquake victims with the necessary materials.
• To date, 400,000 pieces of clothing, hygiene, and food items have been provided from the aid store to 30,000 earthquake victims who came to Ankara Citizen Council building.
• In addition to direct assistance from citizens, around 200 companies and NGOs from Ankara operating in various sectors sent in-kind support.

• Psycho-social support was provided by 8 volunteer psychologists for earthquake victims and their children waiting at Ankara Citizen Council. In this way, support was provided to over 1000 earthquake victims.

• Our Culture and Arts Working Group organized games and various activities throughout the day for earthquake-affected children in the Council building. About 1,000 earthquake-stricken children benefited from the playground created at Ankara Citizen Council.

• In addition to the general needs of earthquake victims, services such as glasses, shoes, and breast milk were provided for people with disabilities and special needs.

• Disinformation and information pollution against the earthquake region and earthquake victims were monitored and timely social media announcements were made to ensure that the entire solidarity and aid process was carried out with accurate communication and information processes.

• Health services were provided for earthquake victims in need of special health care services, and accommodation was provided for earthquake victims close to the place of treatment.

• Companies from Ankara volunteered their support to meet the daily food needs of the volunteers who came together for solidarity at Ankara Citizen Council, and 8,000 meals, pastries, and other foods have been provided so far.

• In addition to Ankara Citizen Council, volunteers from the Capital City Youth Assembly, Tohumluk Foundation, and ABB Sports Club provided support workforce for 1000 people at the aid collection centers of Greater Ankara Municipality and the store established in Altınpark ANFA.

• For the coordination of the disaster solidarity process, coordination meetings were held every day for two weeks with representatives of Ankara Citizen Council and Başkent Youth Assembly. Some 200 volunteers participated in the coordination meetings for face-to-face interaction and 20 hours of work was spent.

• While earthquake solidarity continues, Ankara Citizen Council aims to soon transform its work into a coordination and communication focus in contact with relevant state institutions and organizations.

The Consortium for Sustainable Urbanization (CSU)

The Consortium for Sustainable Urbanization is a New York based, UN Economic and Social Council (ECOSOC) accredited non-for-profit organization 501(c)(3 formed to promote a better understanding of the role of sustainable urbanization and resilient design in the planning of our cities. We connect global thought leaders concerned with urbanization to exchange ideas in high level meetings and public forums. CSU focus is on replicable ideas and concepts, best practices and speculative proposals.

Our purpose is to advocate for responsible and enlightened planning and design. We believe that a cross-sectoral approach can reduce the negative impact of mass migration to cities and improve the quality of life for all. We are committed to make urbanization sustainable.

We work closely with UN-Habitat and UN Department of Economic and Social Affairs (UNDESA) to advance Sustainable Development Goals (SDGs) and advocate for sustainable design and planning, increasing awareness about emerging issues and facilitating knowledge transfer between policymakers, UN delegations, urbanists, architects, academics and activists by catalyzing collaboration, cooperation and coordination to achieve SDGs with particular emphasis on SDG 11 and the New Urban Agenda.

Apart from Green Cities monthly lectures and annual gala, CSU has been organizing flagship Conferences at the UN Headquarters in New York and outside it, lectures and panel meetings with partners, and publishing books.

We disseminate information on-line, in print and in conferences. Our focus is on replicable ideas and concepts, best practices and speculative proposals.

https://csu.global/

About the Authors

Savaş Zafer Şahin, PhD

After graduating from METU (Middle East Technical University) Department of City and Regional Planning, he worked as an urban planner in central and local governments in Turkey. After doing two graduate studies on the relationship between local politics and local governments at The University of Kent in the UK and METU, he wrote his doctoral thesis on the relationship between urban planning and politics in Ankara. He actively participated in civil society activities and the Chamber of City Planners in Ankara. He works as a full-time academician at Ankara Hacı Bayram Veli University. He made significant contributions to public policy-making processes at the national level and received various awards in international and national competitions in the field of urban planning. He has many academic studies published on urban planning, urban transformation, citizen participation, digitalization, urban infrastructure, and conservation of historical areas. He is a member of the German Network of Spatial Sciences (ARL) and the French Institute for Anatolian Studies (IFEA) and participates in international research projects. He has also contributed to developing citizens' assemblies in Turkey for the last 10 years. Since 2019, he has served as the Vice President of The Citizens' Assembly of Ankara. For his contributions to the development of democratic participation in Turkey, he was awarded the "Facilitation Impact Award" in 2020 by the International Association of Facilitators and "Best Practice in Citizen Participation" by the International Observatory on Participatory Democracy (IOPD) in 2021.

Feyzan Erkip, PhD

Photo by Naz Akman

Feyzan Erkip is a retired professor of Bilkent University, Ankara. She taught in the Department of Urban Design and Landscape Architecture and the Department of Interior Architecture and Environmental Design for more than 30 years. Before joining Bilkent University, she worked as a research assistant at Middle East Technical University (METU), where she received her PhD from the Department of City and Regional Planning and the Scientific and

Technological Research Council of Türkiye as researcher.

Her publications appeared in various journals including Progress in Planning, Environment and Planning A, Cities, Journal of Urban Affairs, European Urban and Regional Research, Environment and Behavior, Journal of Environmental Psychology and Third World Planning Review. She was a member of the editorial board of Cities. She carried out research at NYU-Poly during 2011–2012 and at Tilburg University during 2003–2004 academic years as a visiting professor. She received URBAN-NET, Middle East Research Competition and TUBITAK research awards. Her research interests include urban resilience and governance, participatory planning practices, urban transformations and consumption sites, leisure practices and spaces and environmental psychology.

Rick Bell, FAIA

Rick Bell is an Adjunct Associate Professor at Columbia University where he serves as Acting Director of the Center for Buildings, Infrastructure and Public Space. He has worked in six New York mayoral administrations, most recently as Executive Director of Design and Construction Excellence at the Department of Design and Construction, where he was also Chief Architect and Assistant Commissioner of Architecture and Engineering. On leave from DDC, Rick served as Executive Director of the New York Chapter of the American Institute of Architects where he helped establish and animate the Center for Architecture on LaGuardia Place.

After architectural degrees from Yale and Columbia, he worked in offices in New York, France, and Switzerland. A frequent lecturer at architectural conferences, including the UIA in Türkiye in 2005, he is on the advisory board of the NYC Architecture Biennial and chairs the AIA's Delano & Aldrich/Emerson Fellowship. Rick also serves on the board of the Creative Exchange Lab / Center for Architecture + Design STL and on the Summit (NJ) Planning Board. A Fellow of the AIA and Urban Design Forum, Rick is a Chevalier de l'Ordre des Arts et des Lettres, conferred by the French Ministry of Culture and Communication.

Aliye Pekin Çelik, PhD

Aliye P. Celik (Ph.D) has worked in the United Nations DESA as the Chief of Economic and Social Council and Interorganizational Cooperation Branch, Office of ECOSOC Support and Coordination and earlier at the United Nations Programme for Human Settlements (UN-HABITAT) as the Director of the New York office, and as human settlements officer in Nairobi. She was the representative of United Cities and Local Governments to the United Nations. She has B.Arch. and M.Arch degrees from Middle East Technical University, a MFA in Architecture from Princeton University and a Ph.D from

Istanbul Technical University. Celik is a Fulbright scholar and received awards (1997) (2009) (1970) from the American Institute of Architects, SINYC (2006), ICCC (2023) among others. She is the Past President of Soroptimist International New York City and the Consortium for Sustainable Urbanization (CSU), an ECOSOC accredited NGO which she founded with three architects in 2009. She is Chair of the Board of the Consortium for Sustainable Urbanization. She has written extensively on sustainable urbanization, affordable housing, energy conservation and woman and human settlements.

Made in the USA
Columbia, SC
15 December 2023